RIBS

RIBS

*Over 80 all-American
and international recipes
for ribs and fixings*

BY SUSAN R. FRIEDLAND

A Particular Palate Cookbook™
Crown Trade Paperbacks
New York

A Particular Palate Cookbook

The recipe for Red Chile Jam is reprinted with permission from
Jane Butel's Tex-Mex Cookbook, Copyright © 1980 by Jane Butel.

Copyright © 1984, 1996 by Susan R. Friedland

Published by Crown Trade Paperbacks, 201 East 50th Street, New York, New York 10022.
Member of the Crown Publishing Group.

Originally published by Harmony Books, a division of Crown Publishers, Inc. in 1984.

Random House, Inc. New York, Toronto, London, Sydney, Auckland

CROWN TRADE PAPERBACKS, PARTICULAR PALATE and colophons are trademarks of
Crown Publishers, Inc.

Printed in the United States of America

Library of Congress Cataloging-in-Publication Data

Friedland, Susan (Susan R.)

    Ribs.
    1. Cookery (Pork)   I. Title
    TX749.F76   1984
    641.6'64   83-26499
                    CIP

ISBN 0-517-88725-8

10 9 8 7 6 5 4 3 2 1

Second Edition

Contents

Ribs and Fixings/9

Buying and Cooking Ribs/13

Ribs/19

Potatoes, Cornmeal, Beans, and Rice/49

Vegetables/59

Salads/73

Breads and Biscuits/85

Pickles, Relishes, and Chutneys/93

Desserts/101

Index/119

My thanks to all those who generously shared their recipes with me.

For their help, encouragement, enthusiasm, and good appetites I'm particularly grateful to Barbara Appel, Paula Diamond, Gale Goldberg, Marshall Goldberg, Shirley Hochhausen, and Judith Weber.

Ribs and Fixings

Ribs are straightforward, down-home, finger-lickin', all-American food, even when the recipe originates in China or Eastern Europe. Best of all there's no mystery to barbecuing ribs and no special equipment is necessary. City slickers with their simple apartment stoves, as well as suburban folk with their fancy backyard grills, can make better-than-restaurant ribs at home. It's easier to make good ribs than it is to make a good *boeuf bourguignon* or chicken pot pie. In fact, it's hard to make bad ribs. And a meal of ribs and fixings is an event; it's casual fun and people beg to be invited.

The ribs recipes in this book go from barbecued to braised, from Maine to China with stops in Thailand, Texas, and every other place with pigs and cows.

The accompaniments (salads, vegetables, desserts, etc.) are as delicious, and mouthwatering, as the ribs. Most can be prepared in advance and all will elicit "oohs" and "aahs," and "Can I have the recipe?" from your guests.

So plunge right in, try everything, make lots of people happy, and discover America, the melting pot.

Ribs

Buying and Cooking Ribs

To start, you've got to buy the ribs. When spareribs are called for in a recipe, that's what I use and that's what I like best. Buy the meatiest ribs available and remove any loose fat before you start to cook them. You can substitute baby backs or country ribs for most of the spareribs recipes in this book, but I like them less than traditional ribs.

Country ribs aren't ribs at all; they have no bone or only a flimsy one. They are cut from the shoulder end of the loin and though tasty, they don't give the dirty-fingers, greasy-mouth, and crunchy-bone experience that ribs lovers seek. Baby backs simply don't have enough meat on them. Butchers charge a premium for them and the consumer gets less.

Beef short ribs are delicious and meaty. I urge everyone to try them. They require long, slow cooking and are often braised.

When determining quantity, calculate a minimum of one pound of spareribs or short ribs per person. Many guests at my table have eaten one and half to two pounds! Much depends, of course, on your eaters' appetites and what else you're serving. Throughout this book I have used the one-pound-per-person measure.

SAUCES AND MARINADES The sauces and marinades used on ribs contribute heavily to their distinctive and delicious flavor. (The other flavor factor is the fuel you use to cook them.) Every part of the country has its favorite way of preparing ribs. Do not be restrained by regional chauvinism; try different styles and make your own combinations. In Texas, an authentic barbecue has two sauces. The first is the "sop" or "mop," which is a marinade applied to the meat before and during cooking, usually with a small string kitchen mop, hence the name. The sop is saved from one barbecue to the next, growing stronger as it ages. The second sauce is not used in cooking at all but is served as an accompaniment to the meat.

You needn't be as strict as the Texans.

13

Some ribs are delicious served with just the sop in which they were marinated and cooked, without a dipping sauce. If you have leftover marinade, serve it on the side. Not everyone likes to dip. All of the sauces can be made in advance, cooled, and kept refrigerated for 2 or 3 days.

Marinating in either a dry marinade or a composed sauce or soaking the ribs for 3 or 4 hours in 1 cup white vinegar, 2 cups water, and 2 tablespoons salt is the way to start your preparation. Soaking saturates the ribs, which allows longer cooking without burning. This is standard practice in the South. Marinating softens the ribs and imparts a marvelous flavor. If you soak, however, you cannot marinate. Try each; discover your preference. Don't parboil ribs; it toughens them and boils away some of their flavor.

Ribs are juicier when cooked in racks, crisper if you cut them into 2-rib sections before cooking. I prefer to cook them in racks and then cut them into manageable portions just before serving.

COOKING RIBS IN THE OVEN After

you've soaked or marinated, you're ready to cook. You can rely on your kitchen stove for delicious ribs. The best results are yielded by the oven. Preheat the oven to 450° F. Brown the ribs for 30 minutes, without basting, turning once. This will eliminate some of the fat, which will drip into the roasting pan or the pan of water on the bottom of the oven (see below). When the ribs have browned for 30 minutes, lower the oven temperature to 300° F. Cook for another 90 minutes, turning and basting with the sauce or marinade every 15 or 20 minutes. Always use fresh sauce for basting. The sauce in the bottom of the pan will be fatty and probably burned.

The ribs can be cooked on racks in as many roasting pans as are needed and will fit in your oven, or they can be put directly on an oven rack placed in its uppermost position. Place a large shallow pan filled with cold water on the bottom of the oven. The pan will catch the drippings and prevent them from burning. The pan of water and the rack with the ribs must be at least 10 inches apart or the water will steam the ribs and diminish or eliminate the sought-after barbecue taste. Occasionally, you will have to add water to the pan to keep it full.

Do not broil ribs. Broiling toughens them and browning can be accomplished easily in a very hot oven.

GRILLING RIBS If you have a yard, a terrace, or a fireplace, your options for cooking ribs are expanded. Anything from a simple hibachi to an elaborate gas-fired rotisserie will give your ribs an authentic smoky barbecue taste.

Grills come in a variety of shapes and sizes. Braziers are the simplest. They are literally pans for holding coals, and any uncovered or half-hooded grill—among them hibachis, portable picnic grills, fireplace grills, and large grills on legs and/or wheels—falls into this category. On any open brazier the food is cooked by the direct heat generated by the coals. The technique is similar to indoor broiling, though the taste is smoky because of the coals. The same is true of the half-hooded models, which are sometimes equipped with rotisseries. The half-hoods cut down on wind and fire flare-ups.

Covered cookers such as kettle-and-wagon grills are more versatile than uncovered ones. Food, surrounded by uniform heat, is cooked by the heat reflected from the cover as well as by the hot coals. These covered grills work on the same principle as an oven. Heat is adjusted through ventilation, by opening or closing the air vents in the fire pan and the cover.

On gas and electric grills, food is cooked through radiant heat. Permanent lava rocks or ceramic briquettes are heated by the gas flames. These grills are more expensive than braziers or covered grills. Their greatest advantage is the speed with which the fire is started. The fire is also very easily controlled, as easily as a gas stove.

Smoking is a slow, gentle cooking process in which the meat is cooked in a closed chamber with smoke and moisture circulating. Wood smokers can be as simple as two small pans sitting on top of each other. Sawdust or hardwood chips are used to make the fire in the bottom pan. These smokers are simple to use but require careful watching to maintain a constant temperature. Water smokers have a series of three pans. The fire is lit in the bottom one, water is placed in the middle, and the meat on top. When the smoker is covered, steam, flavored by the wood, rises and permeates the meat. No matter what kind of smoker you use, carefully follow the manufacturer's instructions and be sure the smoking is done in a well-ventilated spot. Do not be confident that the smoker has fully cooked the spareribs. After smoking, cooking the ribs for 30 minutes or more in a 350° F. oven is a wise precaution.

The fuel you use for your grill or smoker is important. Only hardwoods should be used because soft woods, such as pine, give off resins that impart an unpleasant, turpentine flavor to the meat. Oak, hickory, alder, and fruitwoods such as apple and cherry have their own distinctive flavor and partisans. Mesquite, a spiny, deep-rooted tree native to the southwestern United States and Mexico, has long been used for smoking and barbecuing in the Southwest. It is now marketed nationally in charcoal or wood-chip form. It is excellent in terms of both flavor and heat, though it does tend to spatter and pop, so take care when you light it.

Your fire can be made from hardwood chips or larger chunks of wood or from charcoal briquettes. These last are made by charring wood in a kiln or retort from which air is excluded. Briquettes made from coal are the least satisfactory, so you should make every effort to find charcoal made from hardwood. Whatever fuel you use, try to avoid starting the fire with kerosene or gasoline: they impart a disagreeable odor to the food that even long, slow cooking doesn't totally eliminate. Electric starters are inexpensive and very effective.

To determine how much fuel you'll need, spread a single layer of wood or charcoal about an inch beyond the edge of the food. To start the fire, stack charcoal or wood in a pyramid. Once the coals or wood have reached the correct temperature, spread them for cooking. Use tongs to add more fuel to the edges of the burning coals every hour to maintain heat. The fire is ready for cooking ribs when the coals are reduced to a gray ash: if you can hold your hand over the coals for more than 2 seconds, the fire isn't hot enough. It will take at least an hour after the fire is started to reach this temperature. Lower the temperature by spreading out the coals or raising the grid; and raise it by tapping ash from the coals or pushing them closer together.

BEVERAGES

Cold, thirst-quenching, and not-too-subtle are the requirements for the beverages that accompany ribs. And beer, cola, or iced tea are what you want. In parts of the South, without ordering, the men are brought beer and the women iced tea, so traditional are those drinks.

The beer and cola will have to be purchased, but the iced tea you should make yourself, from scratch. It's simple to prepare, less expensive than commercial mixes, and has no aftertaste.

Put 4 tea bags or 4 teaspoons loose tea into a clear-glass, quart-size, screw-top jar. Fill the jar with cold tap water, screw on the top, and place in a sunny spot, outdoors or on a windowsill, for a minimum of 3 hours. Sugar, lemon wedges, and sprigs of fresh mint should be served on the side so each drinker can add to taste. One of the advantages of this sun-made tea is that it remains clear and will keep for several days in the refrigerator without getting cloudy.

A nice touch is to serve any of the suggested beverages in frosted glasses. Moisten tall glasses, inside and out, with cold tap water. Shake off any excess water and place the glasses in the freezer for at least 1 hour.

Ribs should not be touched by flames, which will burn the outside but leave the interior raw. They should be cooked by the heat of the ashy coals. The smoke created by the dripping fat and marinade on the coals penetrates the meat, creating the distinctive barbecue taste, which is why the fuel you use is significant. If flames develop in your grill, remove the rack and the ribs together and sprinkle the flames with some baking soda; or, sprinkle water on the coals either with your fingers or a plant mister. Use a minimum amount of water.

There are several techniques for getting smoky-tasting but not burned ribs. If your grill has a cover and air vents, the ribs should be cooked covered for about an hour and then uncovered, 5 or 6 inches from the coals, for 45 minutes to an hour. The cover and the air vents create an oven, fueled by tasty wood or charcoal rather than the utility company.

If you have a grill without a cover, you can make a primitive one with wire hangers and aluminum foil. Clip the hooks off at least 6 wire hangers (the number of hangers you will need depends on the size of your grill) and stretch them out as straight as possible. With 2 or more of the hangers, make a circle, square, or rectangle to fit just inside the grill, twisting the ends together with pliers. With the remaining hangers make a cage having 4 or 5 ribs by attaching one end of each hanger to the circle, square, or rectangle, again using pliers. Fasten the loose ends together at the top with a piece of wire, creating a dome. Cover with aluminum foil, leaving a portion loose at the top to open and close for temperature control.

Or, you can sprinkle the ribs with water, wrap them in a double thickness of aluminum foil and cook, without basting, for 45 minutes to an hour on a rack over the coals. Unwrap the ribs, drain off the fat that will have accumulated in the packets, and put the ribs, brushed with sauce or marinade, on a rack 6 inches from the hot coals for about 30 minutes, turning and basting frequently. The wrapping method yields ribs that are succulent and crisp but not *as* crisp as ribs cooked totally unwrapped on an uncovered brazier.

It's a matter of taste and you'll have to experiment to find your preference.

If you have a rotisserie, thread the ribs accordion fashion on the spit and cook for 1½ to 2 hours, basting frequently.

Finally, if you're cooking on a grill, you'll need two pairs of long tongs—one to turn the meat and the other for arranging the coals—and a pair of heavy-duty pot holders or mitts. The only other bit of equipment you'll need, whether cooking in the oven or on a grill, is a brush for basting.

Ribs

NORTH CAROLINA RIBS

Tom Wicker, a Southerner, reported in the *New York Times* that the "iron law" of barbecue was posted in a Maryland barbecue place owned by a transplanted North Carolinian: "We don't hold with tomatoes." This simple vinegar-based sauce is utterly delicious and the ribs are positively sublime when grilled over hickory chips.

Serves 6

Marinade
1 tablespoon salt
1 tablespoon coarsely ground black pepper
2 teaspoons crushed red pepper flakes

6 pounds spareribs

Sauce
1 cup cider vinegar
8 tablespoons (1 stick) unsalted butter
4 tablespoons brown sugar
2 teaspoons crushed red pepper flakes

1. Combine the marinade ingredients and rub all over the ribs. Marinate for at least 1 hour.

2. Combine the sauce ingredients, bring to a boil, and simmer for 5 minutes. Use the sauce warm for basting the ribs and hot for a dipping sauce.

3. Cook the ribs according to one of the methods described on pages 14–17.

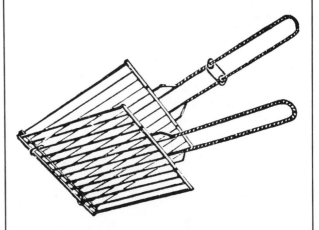

BARBECUE

The word *barbecue*, which can be a noun, a verb, or an adjective, is probably derived from *barbacoa*. Thought to be a word that the Spanish probably picked up from the Arawak Indians, it refers to the green-wood grills set up by the Indians over holes in the ground. Heated stones placed in these holes, or the embers of a fire that was burned down to its glowing coals, were used to cook game or fish. A more colorful but less accurate derivation of the word is that it comes from the French *barbe à queue*, meaning "from whiskers to tail," evoking the image of a whole animal.

HOT BARBECUED RIBS

Serves 6

6 pounds spareribs

1 teaspoon Tabasco
1 cup bottled chili sauce (a brand without
    chemicals, which leave an unpleasant
    aftertaste)
1 teaspoon minced fresh chili (see page 31)
1 tablespoon tarragon vinegar
¼ cup water
¼ cup fresh lemon juice
1 cup chopped onions
1 teaspoon minced garlic
2 teaspoons brown sugar
⅓ cup vegetable oil
½ teaspoon toasted ground cumin seed
1 teaspoon dry mustard
1 teaspoon salt

1. Either soak the ribs (see page 13) for 2 to 4 hours or rub them with a dry marinade (page 29) and let them sit for at least 2 hours or overnight in the refrigerator.

2. Combine all the remaining ingredients in a saucepan. Bring to a boil and simmer for 15 minutes.

3. Put the sauce in a food processor fitted with the metal blade or in a blender; with just two or three on-off motions, the sauce will be the right consistency. It should not be a purée but should retain some texture.

4. Cook the ribs according to one of the methods described on pages 14-17, basting with the sauce. Serve the ribs with the remaining sauce on the side.

To Toast Cumin and Sesame Seeds

Place the seeds in a heavy skillet (cast iron is very good) over moderate heat. Stirring and tossing, toast until the seeds start to pop and take on color. It doesn't take long for the seeds to burn, so pay attention. After toasting, the cumin seeds can be ground in a mortar with a pestle or in an electric coffee or spice mill. The sesame seeds are used whole.

Toast more than you need for any one recipe; the toasted seeds keep well in a dark, airtight jar.

PIGS

Pigs were introduced to America by Hernando de Soto in 1542. When he landed in what is now Tampa, Florida, he had thirteen pigs with him.

SOUTHWESTERN-STYLE RIBS

These ribs are braised and then browned. The sauce penetrates the ribs during the braising and the ribs are served with only that sauce, which clings to them.

Serves 6

Sauce

1 cup chopped onions
2 cups chili sauce (a brand without chemicals, which leave an unpleasant aftertaste)
2 cups ketchup
2 tablespoons Worcestershire sauce
1 tablespoon soy sauce
4 tablespoons fresh lemon juice
2 tablespoons fresh lime juice
½ cup white vinegar
¼ cup brown sugar
4 tablespoons honey
4–6 cloves garlic, mashed
½ teaspoon dry mustard

6 pounds spareribs

1. Combine all the sauce ingredients in a saucepan. Simmer gently for 30 to 45 minutes. The sauce can be made in advance, cooled, and refrigerated for a few days, or it can be used immediately.

2. Preheat the oven to 300° F.

3. Place the ribs in a roasting pan and pour the sauce over them. Make sure all sides and surfaces of the ribs are covered with sauce.

4. Cover the pan with aluminum foil and cook in the preheated oven for 2 hours.

5. Raise the heat to 450° F. Remove the foil and cook the ribs for 30 minutes, turning once. Cut the rack of ribs into 2- or 3-rib sections and serve.

"Many people buy the upper part of the spare-rib of pork, thinking it the most genteel; but the lower part of the spare-rib toward the neck is much more sweet and juicy, and there is more meat in proportion to the bone."
LYDIA MARIA CHILD
The American Frugal Housewife,
1836

RIBS WITH PEANUT SAUCE

This recipe owes a debt to Thai cooking. It is delicious made with both short ribs and spareribs.

Serves 6

Marinade
¾ cup fresh orange juice
⅓ cup fresh lemon juice
2 teaspoons minced garlic
¼ teaspoon sugar
¾ tablespoon soy sauce
Salt
Pepper

6 pounds spareribs

Sauce
3 tablespoons butter
8 heaping tablespoons peanut butter (chunky or smooth)
2 tablespoons soy sauce
2 teaspoons fresh lemon juice
2 teaspoons dried red pepper flakes
½ cup heavy cream

1. Combine all the marinade ingredients in a flat baking dish or roasting pan. Add the ribs, spooning marinade all over them. Marinate for at least 4 hours, or overnight, covered, in the refrigerator.

2. Cook according to one of the methods described on pages 14–17, basting with the marinade.

3. While the ribs are cooking, prepare the sauce by combining in a saucepan the butter, peanut butter, soy sauce, lemon juice, and red pepper flakes. Cook over low heat, stirring, for about 10 minutes. Add the heavy cream and bring just to the simmer. Serve on the side with the ribs.

"Dogs look up at you,
   Cats look down on you,
   But pigs is equal."
   OLD ENGLISH PROVERB

24

CHINESE BARBECUED RIBS

Serves 6

Marinade

6 ounces beer (½ bottle and if it's flat,
    that's okay)
⅓ cup hoisin sauce
⅓ cup soy sauce
⅓ cup honey
⅓ cup minced scallion, including green tops
2 tablespoons minced fresh ginger
2 tablespoons minced garlic
1 tablespoon cider vinegar

6 pounds spareribs

1. Combine all the marinade ingredients in a
small saucepan. Simmer for 5 minutes. Cool
and pour the marinade over the ribs. Marinate for at least 1 hour.

HOISIN SAUCE

Hoisin sauce is made from soy beans, sugar, flour, vinegar, salt, garlic, chilies, and sesame oil. It is reddish-brown in color, has a creamy consistency, and is sweetly pungent. You can purchase it in either glass jars or cans from shops that stock Oriental food. If you buy canned hoisin sauce, transfer what you don't use to a covered jar. It will keep, tightly covered, indefinitely in the refrigerator.

2. Cook according to one of the methods described on pages 14–17, basting with the
sauce only during the last ½ hour of cooking.

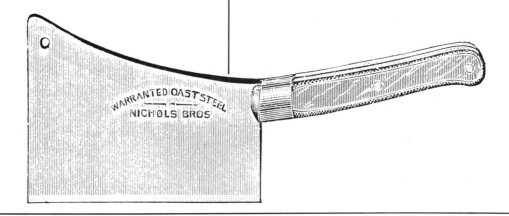

25

MOLASSES BARBECUED RIBS

Serves 6

Soaking Mixture
2 cups water
1 cup white vinegar
2 tablespoons salt

Sauce
2 tablespoons vegetable oil
1 cup chopped onions
¾ cup chopped green pepper
½ – ¾ cup minced celery, including a few
    tablespoons chopped celery leaves
1 tablespoon chopped garlic
2 cups chopped drained canned tomatoes
⅓ cup red wine vinegar
¼ cup unsulfured molasses
2 lemon wedges (each about ⅛ of the whole
    lemon)
½ teaspoon ground cloves
½ teaspoon ground allspice
2 tablespoons tomato paste
1 tablespoon dry mustard
1 teaspoon salt

1. Combine the soaking mixture ingredients and soak the ribs for 2 to 4 hours.

2. Heat the oil in a heavy 10-inch skillet, and over low heat sauté the onions, green pepper, celery, and garlic. Cook until the vegetables are soft, about 10 minutes.

3. Add the remaining ingredients and bring to a boil. Lower the heat and simmer for 30 minutes. The sauce should be thick. Discard the lemon wedges and put the sauce quickly through a food processor fitted with the steel blade. Don't purée the sauce; it should retain a good deal of texture. The blender will homogenize it too much. A good alternative to a food processor is a food mill.

4. Cook the ribs according to one of the methods described on pages 14–17, basting and turning every 15 or 20 minutes. Serve the remaining sauce, heated, with the ribs.

"And the rib, which the Lord God had taken from man, made he a woman."
GENESIS II, 22

JAMES C. WRIGHT'S BARBECUE SAUCE

Congressman Wright (Democrat from Texas) likes to think of himself as a typical Texas barbecuer, and this is his recipe, adapted for ribs. Any leftover sauce should be frozen and used as the basis for the next batch of sauce, taking advantage, as Representative Wright puts it, "of the trickle-down theory."

Serves 6

Marinade
1 cup soy sauce
1 cup fresh lemon juice
1 12-ounce bottle of beer

6 pounds spareribs

Sauce
4 cups tomato juice, V-8 juice, or tomato sauce
½ cup Worcestershire sauce
8 tablespoons (1 stick) unsalted butter
2 cups finely chopped onions
2–4 jalapeño peppers (depending on how hot you like your sauce), seeds removed (see page 31)
2 tablespoons chopped garlic

1. Combine the soy sauce, lemon juice, and 1 cup of the beer in a roasting pan or other vessel large enough to hold the ribs. Marinate, covered, overnight in the refrigerator.

2. Remove the ribs from the marinade and pour the marinade into a heavy saucepan. Add the sauce ingredients, including the remaining ½ cup of beer. Bring the sauce to a boil and simmer gently for at least 3 hours.

3. Cook the ribs according to one of the methods described on pages 14–17, basting with the sauce.

4. While the ribs are cooking, reheat the remaining sauce to serve with the ribs.

LBJ'S BARBECUES

Walter Jetton prepared barbecues for Lyndon Johnson at the LBJ Ranch on the Pedernales River in Texas. Jetton's barbecue sauce consisted of ketchup, cider vinegar, sugar, chili powder, salt, water, celery, bay leaves, garlic, chopped onion, butter, Worcestershire sauce, paprika, and black pepper. The mixture was brought to a boil in vats, simmered briefly, cooled, and served. His sop is a secret.

MISSOURI BARBECUED RIBS

Serves 6

Marinade
2 cups cider vinegar
2 teaspoons freshly ground black pepper
4 teaspoons salt
2 tablespoons brown sugar
2 tablespoons chili powder
2 teaspoons dry mustard
2 teaspoons paprika
2 teaspoons toasted ground cumin seeds (see page 22)
2 tablespoons honey

6 pounds spareribs

1. Combine the marinade ingredients in a large screw-top jar and shake vigorously. Brush the mixture over the ribs and marinate for 4 to 6 hours.

2. Cook according to one of the methods described on pages 14–17, brushing with the sauce every 15 or 20 minutes. Serve remaining sauce, heated, with the ribs.

VIRGINIA RIBS

Mrs. Samuel Tyree of Lynchburg, Virginia, submitted the following recipe for spareribs to the 1879 cookbook, *Housekeeping in Old Virginia:*

"Cut [the spareribs] into pieces of two or three ribs each; put them into a covered stewpan and boil or stew until perfectly done. Just before you take them out add salt, pepper, and minced parsely.

"Put on the cover and simmer until well seasoned.

"Take them out of the pan, drain and dry them.

"For one moment let them scorch on a gridiron over a bed of hot coals; lay on a hot dish; butter each one; pepper added; sift over browned cracker and serve."

EASY RIBS

These ribs are marinated and served with an easy, quickly prepared sauce.

Serves 6

Marinade
1 tablespoon salt
1 tablespoon freshly ground black pepper
2 teaspoons crushed red pepper flakes
4 tablespoons white vinegar

6 pounds spareribs

Sauce
2 cups tomato sauce or ketchup (ketchup makes a sweeter sauce)
8 tablespoons fresh lemon juice
1 teaspoon Louisiana hot sauce or Tabasco
2 tablespoons brown sugar

1. Combine the marinade ingredients and rub into the ribs. Marinate for 1 to 4 hours.

2. Combine the sauce ingredients in a saucepan and simmer gently for 30 minutes.

3. Cook the ribs according to one of the methods described on pages 14–17, brushing with the sauce.

4. Reheat the sauce and serve with the ribs.

GINGER-SOY RIBS

Serves 6

Marinade
¾ cup soy sauce
½ cup maple syrup or honey
½ cup dry sherry
5 garlic cloves, mashed
3 tablespoons grated or finely minced fresh ginger

6 pounds spareribs

1. Combine the marinade ingredients in a small saucepan and boil vigorously for 5 minutes or until the liquid has reduced to 1¼ – 1⅓ cups. Cool and pour over the ribs.

2. Marinate the ribs for at least 4 hours or as long as overnight, covered, in the refrigerator. Turn them in the marinade from time to time.

3. Cook the ribs according to one of the methods described on pages 14–17, basting with the sauce every 15 or 20 minutes. Serve any remaining sauce, heated, with the ribs.

CITRUS-CHILI RIBS

Serves 6

Marinade

2 tablespoons paprika
4 tablespoons salt
1 tablespoon freshly ground black pepper
2 tablespoons dried orange peel, pulverized in a coffee or spice mill (see below)

6 pounds spareribs

Sauce

1 cup bottled chili sauce (a brand without chemicals, which leave an unpleasant aftertaste)
¾ cup brown sugar
1 cup tarragon vinegar
1 tablespoon Worcestershire sauce
1 tablespoon minced parsley
1 teaspoon dry mustard
2 tablespoons fresh lemon juice
½ cup tomato sauce
1 tablespoon dried orange peel, pulverized in a coffee or spice mill (see below)
½ cup olive oil

1. Combine the marinade ingredients and rub all over the ribs. Marinate, in the refrigerator, for 6 hours or overnight.

2. In a saucepan, combine all the sauce ingredients. Bring to a boil and simmer gently for 20 minutes.

3. Cook the ribs, brushed lavishly with sauce, according to one of the methods described on pages 14–17. Serve the ribs with the remaining sauce, heated.

Dried Orange Peel

You can buy dried orange peel or you can easily make your own. Wash the orange and remove the colored part of the rind (the zest) with a potato or vegetable peeler. The white is bitter, so do not use it. Spread the peel on paper towels and leave out on your counter for 3 to 7 days, depending on the humidity. Stored in an airtight jar, it will keep for months.

CITRUS BARBECUED RIBS

Though one rarely has ribs left over, these make a delicious cold snack.

Serves 6

6 pounds spareribs

Sauce

⅓ cup fresh lemon juice
¾ cup fresh orange juice
⅓ cup ketchup or chili sauce
¼ teaspoon chili powder (if you use ketchup)
2 teaspoons prepared white horseradish
1 teaspoon salt
1 tablespoon Worcestershire sauce
Dash of Tabasco
1 tablespoon dry mustard
¼ cup honey or maple syrup
1 tablespoon minced garlic

1. Soak the ribs (see page 13) for 2 to 4 hours.

2. Combine all the ingredients for the sauce in a saucepan but do not heat.

3. Cook the ribs according to one of the methods described on pages 14–17, brushing with the cold sauce during the last 30 minutes of cooking.

4. Heat the remaining sauce to serve with the ribs.

CHILIES

There are an estimated 61 classified varieties of chilies in Mexico alone and even more in the American Southwest. It is thought that South American Indians in Brazil and Peru began eating wild chilies around 6000 B.C. Through the Conquistadors, cultivated chilies were introduced to Spain as early as 1514.

Fresh chilies are generally hotter than dried. In both, it is the seeds that impart the hottest flavor. If you are inexperienced, use few or no seeds at first; then experience will guide you. Serrano, jalapeño, and poblano are the most widely available fresh chilies; serrano is the hottest, poblano the mildest. Chili ancho is a dried version of poblano. Oriental dried red chili and its Latin variety, chili japones, are both very hot.

The heating effect of chili is objectively measurable: growers, dealers, and producers rate it on a scale of 1 to 120. Jalapeño is rated at 15. Imagine a chili rated at 120!

Exercise caution when dealing with chilies. Wear rubber gloves and wash the chilies under cold running water. Use your fingers to remove the seeds. Don't touch your face or eyes. A reflex rub of the eye can cause extreme discomfort and irritation. Thoroughly wash and dry your hands (and the rubber gloves) after dealing with chilies.

PAULA'S RUSSIAN RIBS AND POTATOES

Serves 6

6 pounds spareribs, cut into 2- to 3-rib sections

Marinade
1 teaspoon minced garlic
1 teaspoon hot paprika
½ teaspoon ground allspice
½ teaspoon grated nutmeg
½ teaspoon cinnamon
½ teaspoon cayenne
½ teaspoon freshly grated black pepper
1 teaspoon grated lemon peel
1 tablespoon salt

Stuffed Potatoes
6 large Russet potatoes
1 medium onion
½ pound ground pork
½ pound ground beef
2 eggs
½ cup bread crumbs
1 teaspoon hot paprika
1 teaspoon minced garlic

2–3 pounds beef bones
4 tablespoons apricot jam
Juice of 1 lemon

1. In a small bowl, combine all the marinade ingredients. Rub into the ribs and marinate for at least 1 hour; 3 or 4 hours is best.

2. Peel the potatoes and cut in half across the short dimension. Slice ¼ inch or less off the bottom of each half so it will sit firmly on a flat surface. With a grapefruit knife, scoop out the center of each half, leaving walls about ½ inch thick. Reserve the potato pulp.

3. Put the potatoes you've scooped out along with the onion through a meat grinder or grate in a processor. With your hands, squeeze as much moisture as possible out of the potatoes and onion.

4. Preheat the oven to 350° F.

5. Combine the potato-onion mixture with the ground meats, the eggs, bread crumbs, paprika, and garlic. Fill the potato shells with this mixture, mounding the tops.

6. Arrange the beef bones in the bottom of a large roasting pan. Put the stuffed potatoes on top of the bones and the ribs over and around the potatoes. The pan must be large enough to accommodate everything without crowding. Pour water into the pan to a depth of ½ inch.

7. Cover the pan with aluminum foil and cook for 30 minutes in the preheated oven, basting once with the pan juices. Remove the foil cover, raise heat to 400° F., and continue cooking for 1 hour, until the potatoes are turning brown and the ribs are tender. During the last 15 minutes of cooking, baste the ribs with the apricot jam that has been heated briefly and combined with the lemon juice.

8. To serve, arrange the ribs and potatoes on a platter. Discard the beef bones. Quickly degrease the pan juices, add ½ cup of water and boil briefly, scraping the bottom of the pan. Pour into a sauce boat and serve with the ribs.

MUSTARD RIBS

Serves 6

Marinade
1 tablespoon salt
1 tablespoon freshly ground black pepper
4 tablespoons white vinegar

6 pounds spareribs

Sauce
1 cup ketchup
2 tablespoons cider vinegar
2 tablespoons dry mustard
2 tablespoons soy sauce
1 teaspoon crushed red pepper flakes
1 tablespoon brown sugar

1. Combine the marinade ingredients and rub into the ribs. Marinate for at least 1 hour.

2. In a saucepan combine the ingredients for the sauce, and simmer slowly for 20 minutes. This may be made in advance and reheated just before serving.

3. Cook the ribs according to one of the methods described on pages 14–17, brushing with the sauce during the last 30 minutes.

4. Heat the unused sauce to serve with the ribs.

33

ARIZONA BARBECUED RIBS

Serves 6

Marinade
4 teaspoons salt
½ teaspoon freshly ground black pepper
2 teaspoons paprika
6 cloves garlic, chopped
½ cup fresh lemon juice
1 small onion, chopped

6 pounds spareribs

Sauce
½ cup bacon drippings
1 cup finely chopped onions
½ cup finely chopped celery
½ cup chopped tomatoes, fresh or canned
½ cup tomato sauce
½ teaspoon dry mustard
2 tablespoons Worcestershire sauce
1 cup cider vinegar
2 tablespoons brown sugar
2 fresh jalapeño or other hot green chilies, seeded and chopped (about 1 tablespoon) (see page 31)
1 teaspoon toasted ground cumin seeds (see page 22)
1 teaspoon dried thyme

1. Combine the salt, pepper, and paprika and rub all over the ribs.

2. Combine the garlic and lemon juice and pour over the spareribs. Scatter the chopped onions over the ribs. Make sure the ribs are well coated. Marinate overnight or for at least 6 hours, turning from time to time.

3. Heat the bacon drippings in a heavy skillet, and sauté the onions and celery for about 10 minutes, or until soft. Add the remaining ingredients and simmer for 20 minutes.

4. Cook the ribs according to one of the methods described on pages 14–17, brushing frequently with the sauce during the cooking.

5. Heat remaining sauce to serve with the ribs.

PIGS

Pork is the world's leading meat because it's so economical. Pigs will eat virtually anything (though the better they eat, the better the meat tastes) and are capable of finding their own food when man does not provide it. There is hardly any waste in the pig; almost all of it can be eaten and its nonedible parts have value: its skin is used for leather; its glands have pharmaceutical uses; its stomach produces pepsin; and its hair is used in upholstery and insulation. There was truth as well as humor in the Chicago meat packer's slogan: "We use everything but the oink."

CROWN ROAST OF SPARERIBS

Serves 8–10

6 pounds spareribs, 2 large racks, each 12–15
    inches long and 4–6 inches high
2 teaspoons crumbled dried sage
2 teaspoons minced garlic
1 tablespoon kosher salt
2 teaspoons coarsely ground black pepper
1 pound sweet pork sausage
3 cups chopped onions
1 cup chopped celery
10–15 cloves garlic, peeled and chopped
2 cups chopped tart apples, peeled and cored
2 cups long-grain rice
2 cups chicken broth
½ teaspoon crushed fennel seed
½ teaspoon thyme
Salt
4 tablespoons unsalted butter, melted
4 tablespoons white wine

1. Wipe the ribs with a damp cloth. If there is loose meat at the narrow end, cut it off and chop finely or grind in a meat grinder and reserve for step 4.

2. In a small bowl, combine the sage, garlic, salt, and pepper. Rub into the ribs and set aside to marinate.

3. Prick the skin of the sausage and sauté in a large heavy skillet until brown, about 20 minutes. Remove the sausage to a mixing bowl, leaving the fat in pan. When the sausage is cool enough to handle, take off the casing and mash the meat with a fork.

4. In the fat in the skillet, sauté the onions, celery, garlic, apples, and any chopped or ground meat trimmed from the ribs. Cook, stirring occasionally, for 15 minutes.

5. Add the rice to the skillet. Stir to coat with the vegetables and apples. Add the chicken broth and 2 cups of water or 4 cups water only, fennel seed, thyme, salt and pepper to taste. Stir, bring to a boil, lower heat, cover skillet, and cook gently for 15 minutes, or until the rice is tender. Combine in the mixing bowl with the cooked sausage.

6. Preheat the oven to 375° F.

7. Stand the ribs in a roasting pan with the bonier side facing in. Sew or skewer the racks together and fill the center with the stuffing.

8. Roast in the preheated oven for 2 hours, basting the outside 2 or 3 times with the melted butter and wine. If the stuffing or ribs start to burn, cover with foil.

9. To serve, transfer the roast to a large platter using 2 spatulas or flat wooden paddles. Remove the skewers or thread *after* your guests have admired the roast. Transfer the stuffing to a bowl, cut the rack into 2-rib sections, and serve.

SPARERIBS AND SAUERKRAUT CASSEROLE

This classic American dish cooks for about 5 hours, but the cooking can be interrupted and the entire casserole can be made in advance and reheated. When reheating, bring the casserole to a simmer on top of the stove before putting in the oven.

Serves 6–8

2 pounds sauerkraut (fresh or in plastic bags, *not* canned)
8 slices (6 ounces) bacon
1½ cups finely chopped onions
1 cup thinly sliced carrots
½ cup chopped celery
2 teaspoons chopped garlic
6 parsley sprigs
1 bay leaf, crumbled
4 whole cloves
8 whole black peppercorns
10 juniper berries, crushed (or pour 3 or 4 tablespoons gin directly into the pot)
6 pounds spareribs
2 cups dry white wine
2–3 cups chicken or beef stock

1½ pounds potatoes, peeled and thinly sliced
1½–2 pounds tart apples, peeled, cored, and minced (4–5 cups)

1. Put the sauerkraut in a colander and rinse in cold, running water to remove some of the brine and, if it isn't fresh, some of the preservatives. Let the water run over the sauerkraut while you prepare the vegetables and bacon.

2. Blanch the bacon in boiling water for 2 minutes. Drain, dry on paper towels, chop, and sauté in a large casserole for a few minutes, until the bacon browns and releases some of its fat.

3. Preheat the oven to 300° F.

4. Add the onions, carrots, celery, and garlic to the bacon. Cover the casserole and cook for 10 to 15 minutes.

5. Drain the sauerkraut, squeeze out as much water as you can, and pull apart to separate the strands. Add to the casserole and stir sauerkraut, coating it with the fat and vegetables.

6. In a piece of cheesecloth, tie together the parsley, bay leaf, cloves, peppercorns, and crushed juniper berries (if used). Bury this herb bouquet in the sauerkraut. Add the wine and 2 cups of the broth. Bring to a boil on top of the stove, cover the casserole, and place in the preheated oven for 2½ hours.

7. If you have two ovens, brown the ribs on a rack in a roasting pan at 450 degrees for 30 minutes, turning once while the sauerkraut is cooking. This process gives the ribs a good color and removes some of the fat. If you have one oven, wait until the sauerkraut has cooked for the 2½ hours, remove it, raise the oven temperature, and brown the ribs. Reset the oven to 300° F.

8. When the sauerkraut has cooked for 2½ hours and the ribs are browned, stir the apples and potatoes into the casserole, add the ribs, cover, and cook for another 2 hours. If all the liquid has been absorbed, add ½ to 1 cup broth; there should be an inch or two on the bottom of the pan when you add the ribs. Finally, remove the cover, raise the temperature to 375° F., and cook for an additional hour. Serve piping hot.

BLACK PEPPER

Chili and cayenne, paprika and bell peppers, all *Capsicum,* were misnamed by Christopher Columbus, who thought he had found Asia, the land of pepper, when he sailed into the Caribbean. He called the hot spice served him by the Indians pepper, and the name stuck.

Columbus was looking for the *Piper nigrum,* the world's most important and widely used spice since ancient times. Hippocrates cited pepper as medicine. Plato said it is "small in quantity and great in virtue." Ancient Rome saved itself from Attila the Hun in 452 by giving him gifts, among them pepper and cinnamon.

Pepper grows on a vine equipped with tendrils with which it clings to a tree for support. It grows best 10 to 15 degrees from the equator in high temperatures, partial shade, and a long rainy season. The grains are picked unripe, just before they begin to redden from their green state (a culinary treat introduced to the West after World War II). They are then dried, preferably in the sun; in a few days they turn black and are ready for shipping. For white pepper, the grains ripen on the vine, are picked, and soaked in water to loosen the outer skin, which is rubbed off. These are also dried, but they don't blacken without the skin. White peppercorns are more expensive than black ones because of the extra work involved and because of the weight loss (and thereby financial loss to the growers and shippers) without their skins.

Black pepper is native to southeast India, from whose Malabar-coast port of Tellicherry the best peppercorns are still shipped, though India has been displaced in quantity of production by Indonesia.

STUFFED SPARERIBS

This sort of ribs sandwich is an unusual and very tasty variation. Though the recipe jumps around a bit, this sequence makes the most efficient use of your time.

Serves 6

Marinade
2 tablespoons paprika
3 tablespoons salt
1 tablespoon freshly ground black pepper
2 tablespoons dried orange peel, pulverized in a coffee or spice mill (see page 30)
6 pounds spareribs, in 2 racks of roughly equal size

Stuffing
½ pound dried apricots
½ cup diced celery
1 cup chopped onions
4 tablespoons unsalted butter
2 tart apples, peeled, cored, and chopped
2 cups crumbled leftover corn bread, or fresh bread crumbs

Sauce
2 cups orange juice
½ cup vinegar
4 tablespoons lemon juice
2 teaspoons grated lemon peel
½ cup raisins
½ cup pure maple syrup
Nutmeg
½ cup gingersnap crumbs

1. Combine the marinade ingredients in a small bowl. Rub into the ribs and marinate for 3 to 6 hours.

2. Preheat the oven to 450° F.

3. Pour 1 cup boiling water over the apricots and let soak for 20 to 30 minutes.

4. Put the ribs, meaty side up, on a rack in a roasting pan. Brown on one side only in the hot oven for 15 to 20 minutes. Remove the ribs and reduce the oven heat to 350° F.

5. Sauté the celery and onions slowly in the butter for 15 minutes, stirring. Add the apples and cook 5 minutes more.

6. Remove the apricots from the soaking liquid and chop them. Reserve the liquid.

7. In a saucepan, combine the orange juice, vinegar, lemon juice, lemon peel, raisins, maple syrup, a few gratings of nutmeg, and the gingersnap crumbs. Simmer, stirring, for 10 minutes, or until the sauce is thick. Set aside.

8. In a mixing bowl, combine the corn bread or bread crumbs, the sautéed vegetables, the apricots, and ½ cup of the apricot soaking liquid. The stuffing should be roughly the consistency of damp sand; if it seems too dry, add more apricot liquid.

9. Brush the unbrowned side of one rack of ribs with the sauce and place, sauce side down, on a rack in a roasting pan. Spread the stuffing in a thick mound—higher in the middle than on the sides—over the browned side of that rack and cover with the other rack, placing its browned side on the stuffing. Skewer together or tie with kitchen string. Baste the top and sides with the sauce.

10. Place the ribs in the 350° F oven and cook for 90 minutes, basting with the sauce 2 or 3 times during the cooking.

11. Serve the ribs with the extra sauce, heated.

MAPLE BARBECUED RIBS

Though it's expensive, you should use 100 percent pure maple syrup in this recipe. Its smoky taste cannot be duplicated with the product sold as pancake syrup, which is really 95 to 97 percent corn syrup.

Serves 6

Marinade
2 tablespoons salt
2 tablespoons freshly ground black pepper
2 tablespoons white vinegar

6 pounds spareribs

Sauce
1 cup maple syrup
2 tablespoons bottled chili sauce (a brand without chemicals, which leave an unpleasant aftertaste)
2 tablespoons cider vinegar
2 tablespoons minced onions
½ teaspoon dry mustard

1. Combine the marinade ingredients and rub all over the ribs. Marinate for at least 1 hour, at the most 4 hours.

2. Combine all the sauce ingredients in a saucepan.

3. Before cooking according to one of the methods described on pages 14–17, wipe off most of the marinade. Baste the ribs frequently with the sauce during cooking and heat the remainder to serve with the ribs.

ORIENTAL SWEET-AND-SOUR APPETIZER SPARERIBS

These ribs can be prepared several hours in advance, through step 5. Make sure they cool in a single layer, without touching. Crammed together, the fried ribs will steam and become soggy.

Serves 6

1½ pounds spareribs
4 tablespoons soy sauce
1 tablespoon dry sherry
Peanut oil for frying
½ cup plus 2 teaspoons cornstarch
3 tablespoons sugar
3 tablespoons cider or white vinegar
3 scallions, including green tops, chopped
1 tablespoon Oriental sesame oil

1. Cut the rack of spareribs into individual ribs. One at a time, cut each rib into 1-inch pieces. This will take a strong hand and a sharp cleaver. An unconventional but effective alternative is to use a knife and hammer: hold the knife in position on the rib and give it a whack with the hammer.

2. Combine the soy sauce and sherry. Marinate the ribs in the mixture for at least 30 minutes.

3. In a large, heavy skillet or wok, add peanut oil to a depth of ½ inch and heat to 350° F. (In a 10-inch cast-iron skillet, you will need 3 cups of oil.) To test, a bread cube should fry to a golden color in about 40 seconds.

4. Place ½ cup of the cornstarch in a paper bag. Remove the ribs from the marinade, reserving the marinade, and put the ribs in the bag with the cornstarch. Vigorously shake the bag. With your hand in the bag to avoid unnecessary mess, shake each rib to remove excess cornstarch. They should be only lightly coated.

5. Fry a few ribs at a time for 3 or 4 minutes, tossing and turning with a slotted spoon so they cook evenly. Do not crowd the pan. Remove the ribs to paper towels and cool for a few minutes. Return the ribs to the hot oil for an additional minute or two. The ribs should be a deep brown, but take care not to burn them. Remove the ribs from the oil and drain again on paper towels. Discard the oil and wipe out the skillet with paper towels.

6. Dissolve the remaining 2 teaspoons cornstarch in 3 tablespoons cold water. Add to the reserved marinade along with the sugar, vinegar, scallions, and sesame oil.

7. Heat 1 tablespoon fresh peanut oil in the skillet or wok. Pour in the sauce and, stirring constantly, bring to a boil. Add the spareribs and cook, stirring to coat them, until the ribs are thoroughly heated. Serve immediately with toothpicks and lots of napkins.

BOURBON RIBS

Serves 6

Marinade
½ cup soy sauce
8 tablespoons bourbon
4 tablespoons brown sugar
2 teaspoons minced garlic

6 pounds spareribs

1. Combine all the marinade ingredients and marinate the ribs in the sauce for at least 1 hour. Spoon the marinade over tops and sides of the ribs and turn a couple of times. If you have time, marinate the ribs in the refrigerator for 4 to 6 hours.

2. Bring the ribs to room temperature before cooking according to one of the methods described on pages 14–17, brushing frequently with the marinade.

ALABAMA BARBECUES
In Alabama, some people start drinking a bottle of bourbon when they start the fire and claim the ribs are done when the bottle is emptied.

KOREAN SHORT RIBS (BULKOGI)

Serves 6–8

Marinade

½ cup toasted sesame seeds (see page 22)
4 tablespoons minced garlic
⅔ cup soy sauce
4 tablespoons grated fresh ginger
2 teaspoons sugar
4 tablespoons Oriental sesame oil
4 tablespoons water
1 cup chopped scallions, including green tops

6 pounds short ribs, cut into 2- to 3-inch
    pieces

1. In a large nonaluminum bowl or pot, combine all the marinade ingredients and mix well.

2. Add the ribs, making sure all sides of each piece are fully coated with marinade. Cover and refrigerate for at least 8 hours or overnight.

3. Preheat the oven to 375° F. or start a fire in the grill.

4. Remove the ribs from the marinade and place them on a rack in a roasting pan or 6 inches above the hot white embers of the grill. Turn and baste the ribs every 15 minutes or so for 1 to 1½ hours. Cut into a rib to test for doneness; unlike pork, these can be served rare.

SHORT RIBS

our seasoned

is very good
or bacon fat.
batches. Do not
ll steam rather
drain the ribs

h to hold the
t-fitting cover,
er. Add the
ok very slowly
ilted but not
s.

the onions.
beef stock.

simmer on top
n for about 1
nding upon the
en done should
fork.

and refrigerate
and rise to the
. Reheat the
e serving. If
igerate the
you can before

the

y,

h

1. Place the ribs in a large bowl or roasting pan. Combine all the marinade ingredients and pour over the ribs. Marinate overnight in the refrigerator, covered.

2. Transfer the meat and marinade to a heavy pot with a tight-fitting lid. Bring to a boil, cover the pan, and simmer for 2 to 3 hours. The meat should be very tender, almost falling off the bone.

3. Strain the liquid into a bowl, cool slightly, and refrigerate, uncovered. The fat will rise to the top and harden and can easily be removed. This will take at least 3 hours.

4. Reheat before serving.

BRAISED SHORT RI

These are utterly delicious: tender, flavorful, succulent. They can be made in advance and, indeed, improve if you do so.

Serves 6–7

6 pounds short ribs, cut into 2- to 3-inch
    pieces
Flour
Salt
Freshly ground black pepper
3 tablespoons vegetable oil or bacon fat
2 tablespoons butter plus 2 tablespoons vege-
    table oil
4 cups chopped onions
1 tablespoon chopped garlic
2 teaspoons dried thyme
2 teaspoons dried rosemary
1½ cups beef stock or broth (don't use
    canned consommé)

1. Lightly dredge the ribs in
with salt and pepper.

2. In a heavy skillet (cast iro
for this), heat the vegetable o
Brown the ribs on all sides in
crowd the skillet or the ribs w
than brown. As they are done
on paper towels.

3. In a pan that is large enou
ribs comfortably *and* has a tig
heat the vegetable oil and bu
chopped onions and garlic. C
until the onions are soft and
brown, about 15 or 20 minut

4. Place the drained ribs ove
Add the thyme, rosemary, an

5. Bring to a boil, cover, and
of the stove or in a 300° F. ov
hour. It may take longer, dep
quality of the meat, which wh
be tender when pierced with

6. If you have the time, strai
the juices. The fat will harde
top and can easily be remove
dish for 15 or 20 minutes bef
you don't have the time to re
juices, skim off as much fat a
serving.

SPICY SHORT RIBS

These ribs are delicious when barbecued on the grill.

Serves 6

1 cup chopped onions
1 cup chopped celery
1 teaspoon minced garlic
4 tablespoons unsalted butter
3 tablespoons brown sugar
3 tablespoons cider vinegar
1 cup ketchup
1 cup beef broth (don't use canned
    consommé)
1 teaspoon Worcestershire sauce
2 teaspoons Dijon mustard
Salt
Freshly ground black pepper
2 small dried chilies (Japones or Oriental),
    seeded and chopped or pounded in a
    mortar with a pestle (see page 31)
1 tablespoon fresh lemon juice

6 pounds short ribs, cut into 2- to 3-inch
    pieces

1. Slowly sauté the onions, celery, and garlic in the butter until the vegetables are soft but not browned, about 10 minutes.

2. Add the sugar and vinegar. Stir for a moment or two before adding the ketchup, beef broth, Worcestershire sauce, mustard, salt, pepper, and chilies. Simmer the mixture slowly for 25 to 30 minutes. Stir in the lemon juice and let the sauce cool. You should have about 3 cups of marinade.

3. Put the ribs in a shallow roasting pan and pour the marinade over. Make sure all sides of the meat are coated. Marinate for 4 to 6 hours, turning occasionally and coating with the marinade.

4. Start a fire in the grill about 2 ½ hours before you plan to serve the ribs. The fire will take at least an hour to reach the gray-ash stage and the ribs should cook for approximately 1 ½ hours. While the ribs are grilling, turn frequently so all sides get crisp, basting with the sauce each time you turn. Cut into a rib to test for doneness.

SHORT RIBS WITH VINEGAR AND CAPER SAUCE

Serves 6

6 pounds short ribs, cut into 2- to 3-inch
    pieces
Salt
Freshly ground black pepper
4 tablespoons lard or vegetable oil
8 cups coarsely chopped onions
1 cup wine vinegar
1 bay leaf
½ teaspoon ground cloves
½ teaspoon marjoram
6 tablespoons capers
6 tablespoons fresh bread crumbs
1 teaspoon grated lemon peel

1. Sprinkle the ribs generously with salt and pepper.

2. Heat the lard or vegetable oil in a large heavy skillet. Add the ribs and brown on all sides, regulating the heat so the lard doesn't burn. Don't crowd the pan; in a 12-inch skillet you'll need to fry in 2 batches. As the ribs are browned, remove to a plate.

3. Add the onions to the skillet and cook, stirring, for 10 minutes, until they are soft. Add ½ cup of vinegar, raise the heat, and boil off most of the vinegar, scraping the bottom of the pan with a wooden spoon to dislodge any stuck bits of meat or onion.

4. Add the bay leaf, cloves, marjoram, the ribs, and enough water to come ⅔ the way up the sides of the ribs—3 or 4 cups. Cover the skillet, reduce heat, and simmer for 90 minutes.

5. Remove the ribs to a plate. Skim off all the fat and discard the bay leaf. If you have the time, strain the liquid into a bowl and refrigerate. In a few hours the fat will harden at the top and be easy to remove. Reheat before continuing.

6. Stir into the skillet the capers with a bit of their liquid, bread crumbs, the remaining ½ cup of vinegar, and the lemon peel. Bring to a boil, reduce heat, and simmer for 5 minutes. Pour the sauce over the meat and serve.

DEVILLED SHORT RIBS

Serves 6

6 pounds short ribs, cut into 2- to 3-inch
    lengths

Marinade
½ cup chopped onions
⅔ cup lemon juice
⅔ cup olive oil
5 tablespoons strong mustard (English or
    Dijon)
2 tablespoons minced garlic
Tabasco
Salt
Freshly ground black pepper

1–1 ½ cups coarse fresh bread crumbs

Mustard Sauce
Makes 2 cups

4 tablespoons unsalted butter
1 cup chopped onions
2 tablespoons flour
2 cups beef broth or stock (*not* consommé)
1 tablespoon prepared white horseradish
4 tablespoons strong mustard (English or
    Dijon)

1. In a roasting pan or other large flat pan, combine onions, lemon juice, olive oil, mustard, garlic, a dash of Tabasco, salt, and pepper. Add the short ribs and coat them thoroughly. Marinate for 4 hours or overnight, turning occasionally.

2. Preheat the oven to 350° F.

3. Put the ribs on a rack in a roasting pan and cook in the preheated oven for 1 ¼ to 1 ½ hours, turning and basting with the marinade 2 or 3 times. Recipe can be prepared several hours in advance to this point. Leave uncovered and unrefrigerated.

4. Raise the oven to 450° F.

5. Baste the ribs one last time with the marinade so the crumbs will adhere easily. Put the bread crumbs on a plate and roll the ribs in them to coat thoroughly. (Recipe can also be prepared to this point and set aside, uncovered and unrefrigerated for a few hours.) Place in the hot oven for 20 minutes, turning once.

6. To make the sauce, melt the butter in a heavy saucepan and add the onions. Cook gently for 10 minutes. Stir in the flour and, stirring constantly, cook for 3 minutes. Gradually add the stock, stirring all the while so the sauce will be smooth. Simmer gently for 10 minutes. Add the horseradish and mustard, stir, and serve with the ribs.

TZIMMES

Tzimmes, a dish of spiced and sweetened vegetables, fruit, and meat, has as many variations as there are cooks who prepare it. This version, originally my mother's, was expanded by my cousin Barbara.

Because of the great variety of ingredients that must be scrubbed, peeled, sliced, diced, and simmered, the Yiddish word tzimmes has become synonymous with a complicated chore or unnecessary fuss. (The fuss is only unnecessary in the nonculinary use of the word; the tzimmes itself is worth every bit of preparation.) It is a very rich and filling dish.

Serves 8–10

Vegetable oil
Salt
Freshly ground black pepper
6 pounds lean, meaty flanken (short ribs, 6–
    10 inches long, from the plate section)
4 cups chopped onions
1 pound pitted tart prunes
11 ounces dried apricots
2½ pounds carrots, scraped and sliced
2 pounds sweet potatoes, peeled and sliced
1 lemon
½ teaspoon ground cloves
2 teaspoons grated fresh ginger
½ teaspoon ground cinnamon
Nutmeg

1. Film the bottom of a large heavy pot with vegetable oil. Salt and pepper the meat and brown in the heated oil, in batches to avoid crowding the pot and steaming the meat. Add the onions and cook until soft. Cover the pot and cook the meat and onions for 1 hour over very gentle heat.

2. Pour 4 cups boiling water over the prunes and the apricots and let soak for 30 minutes.

3. Preheat oven to 325° F.

4. After the meat has cooked for an hour, add the prunes and apricots and their soaking liquid to the pot, along with the carrots, sweet potatoes, juice and grated peel of the lemon, cloves, ginger, cinnamon, and a few gratings of nutmeg. Replace the cover and cook the tzimmes for 2½ to 3 more hours in the preheated oven. During the last 30 to 45 minutes, remove the cover; the top of the tzimmes should brown lightly.

Any leftover tzimmes can be frozen. Defrost in the refrigerator before reheating in a 325° F. oven.

Potatoes, Cornmeal, Beans, and Rice

FRIED POTATOES IN THEIR SKINS

These are not your standard French fries: the skin is included and the fries are disc shaped. Baking the potatoes before frying dries them out thoroughly and results in crisper fries.

Serves 6–8

7–8 Idaho potatoes
Vegetable oil
Salt

1. Preheat the oven to 375° F.

2. Scrub the potatoes, rub lightly with vegetable oil, and puncture each potato in one or two places with a fork.

3. Bake in the preheated oven for 45 minutes.

4. When cool enough to handle, make ¼-inch-thick round slices, cutting across the potato (that is, across the short dimension). Each slice will be rimmed with skin.

5. In a heavy skillet, heat about ½ inch of oil. Fry the potato slices until golden brown, turning once. Don't crowd the skillet or the potatoes won't brown properly.

6. Sprinkle with salt and serve immediately.

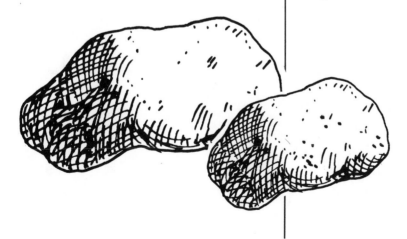

LEMON POTATOES

These potatoes go very well with spicy ribs. They can be prepared in advance up to the final baking.

Serves 6

3 pounds potatoes (baking or all-purpose)
1 teaspoon grated lemon peel
5 tablespoons unsalted butter
6 tablespoons chopped parsley
4 tablespoons chopped onions
3 tablespoons chopped chives
Salt
Freshly ground black pepper
Nutmeg
2 tablespoons fresh lemon juice

1. Preheat the oven to 350° F.

2. Peel and cube the potatoes. Cook them in boiling salted water to cover for 10 minutes. Drain the potatoes and put them back in the pot in which they cooked. Shake the pot for a moment or two over moderate heat to dry the potatoes.

3. Off the heat, toss the potatoes with the lemon peel, dots of the butter, parsley, onions, chives, salt, pepper, and a few gratings of nutmeg.

4. Turn the potatoes into a buttered casserole and bake in the preheated oven for 20 to 30 minutes or until tender.

5. Sprinkle the lemon juice over the potatoes just before serving.

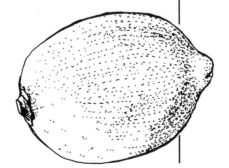

STUFFED POTATOES

These potatoes can be prepared several hours in advance of serving. The final and easiest step is done just before serving. Frying the skins before stuffing adds unexpected crunch and the delicious taste of bacon fat. You can, however, skip that step and still have very good potatoes. Or, you can skip stuffing the potatoes and serve just the fried skins.

Serves 6–8

6 medium-size Idaho potatoes
Vegetable oil
½ pound bacon, diced
1½ cups grated sharp Cheddar cheese (about 6 ounces)
4 tablespoons unsalted butter

1. Preheat the oven to 375° F.

2. Scrub the potatoes, rub them lightly with vegetable oil, and puncture each with a fork in one or two places. Bake on a rack in the preheated oven for 1 hour.

3. In a small, heavy skillet, sauté the bacon. Drain on paper towels, leaving the fat in the pan for (optional) step 6.

4. When the potatoes are cool enough to handle, slice them in half lengthwise. Using a spoon, carefully remove most of the interior, leaving a thin layer of potato attached to the skin. The skin should remain intact. Place the potatoes in a mixing bowl.

5. Add the sautéed bacon, cheese, and butter to the potatoes, and mash together with a fork or a potato masher.

6. (Optional) Heat the bacon fat in the skillet and add the potato-skin shells, being careful not to crowd the skillet. Maneuvering with two chopsticks or wooden spoons, fry all surfaces of the skins, taking care not to tear or puncture them. The skins will stiffen and the potato left in the skins will turn brown. Remove the skins from the skillet and drain on paper towels.

7. Stuff the potato mixture back into the shells. You can prepare them up to this point in advance.

8. When ready to serve, place the stuffed potatoes in the preheated 350° F. oven for 5 to 10 minutes or until hot.

MASHED POTATOES

These are not conventional mashed potatoes because the skin is included, giving an interesting and unusual texture to the finished dish. To prevent the potatoes from turning hard and lumpy while waiting to be served keep them in a double boiler over simmering water, stirring from time to time. They will retain their creamy texture for about 30 minutes.

Serves 6

6 large Idaho potatoes
6 tablespoons unsalted butter, softened
8 tablespoons heavy cream, light cream, or
     milk
Salt
Freshly ground black pepper
Nutmeg
2–3 tablespoons chopped chives or parsley

1. Preheat the oven to 350° F.

2. Scrub the potatoes, pierce with a fork in one or two places (to prevent possible explosion), and place in the preheated oven. Bake for 1 hour.

3. When the potatoes are cool enough to handle, quarter them and put them through a food mill or potato ricer. Any skin that does not go through the food mill will have to be chopped by hand or put in a food processor fitted with the steel blade.

4. Put the potatoes in the top of a double boiler placed over simmering water. Add the butter, cream or milk, salt, pepper, and a few gratings of nutmeg. Stir until the butter is totally melted and the potatoes are hot.

5. Served sprinkled with chopped chives or parsley.

POTATO CAKES. Leftover mashed potatoes are delicious when fried. You may even want to make mashed potatoes expressly for this purpose and not risk being without leftovers.
   Beat an egg or two into the potatoes (skin, chives, and all). Form into patties 2 or 3 inches in diameter, roll in bread crumbs or cornflakes, and fry in butter, turning once. Regulate the heat so the butter doesn't burn.

CORNMEAL MUSH

This is a hearty and satisfying accompaniment to ribs; it is also the basis for the other cornmeal dishes that follow. Cornmeal mush is the original Hasty Pudding, served in Yankee households with maple syrup.

Serves 6–8

5 cups water
1½ cups yellow cornmeal
2 teaspoons salt
8 tablespoons (1 stick) unsalted butter
1 cup grated hard cheese (such as Parmesan, Gruyère, or sharp Cheddar)

1. Bring the water to a boil in the top of a double boiler.

2. Gradually stir (or slowly sift through a strainer) the cornmeal into the boiling water. Stir slowly and constantly to avoid lumps. If lumps do develop, mash them with the backs of two wooden spoons. Add salt and boil for 5 minutes, stirring.

3. Cover, place over simmering water, and cook for 45 minutes to 1 hour, until all the water is absorbed.

4. Stir in the butter and cheese and serve immediately. Or turn the mixture into a loaf pan to cool. Refrigerate, covered, if you plan to hold for more than half a day.

FRIED CORNMEAL MUSH. Cut the cool, firm mush into slices approximately ¾ inch thick. Fry the slices in hot butter or bacon fat until brown and crisp. Or dip the slices in a batter made with 1 egg yolk beaten with 2 tablespoons milk, then in fine bread crumbs. This is very good served with maple syrup.

CORNMEAL

Corn is the only grain native to North America. It was widely used by the Indians before Columbus. Cornmeal is made simply of ground corn kernels. Water- or stone-ground cornmeal retains the germ, which is rich in vitamins; commercially ground meal is made from only the starchy part of the kernel. The texture of the meal can range from coarse to fine, and different dishes require different textures. The difference between yellow and white cornmeal is only color, with the North favoring yellow and the South white.

If you can find water- or stone-ground cornmeal, by all means use it. If it's unavailable, use the commercially ground cornmeal found in your supermarket.

HOPPIN' JOHN

Black-eyed peas are the basis of a legendary southern dish known as hoppin' John. It is traditionally served on New Year's Day, in cabins as well as great plantations. A coin buried in the beans is supposed to bring good luck to the one in whose portion it is found.

Serves 8

2 cups black-eyed peas (frozen, canned, or dried)
½ pound bacon or salt pork
1 cup chopped onions
½ cup chopped celery, including a few tablespoons of chopped leaves
1 bay leaf
Pinch cayenne or crushed red pepper flakes
Salt
Freshly ground black pepper
1 cup long-grain rice
Chopped parsley

1. If you are using dried peas, soak them overnight in cold water to cover and then drain. Or place the beans in a saucepan, cover with water, bring to a boil, and let stand, off the heat and covered, for 2 hours; then drain. Canned peas should be drained and rinsed in cold water until the liquid runs clear. Frozen peas can be used directly from the freezer.

2. Dice the bacon or salt pork and brown in a skillet. Pour off all but 2 tablespoons of the fat. Add the onions and celery and sauté for 3 or 4 minutes. The dish can be prepared up to this point and set aside for several hours.

3. To the skillet, add the peas, 2 cups fresh cold water, bay leaf, cayenne, salt, and pepper.

4. Bring to a simmer, cover the pan, and cook gently for 30 minutes. Add the rice and cook for another 15 to 20 minutes. You may need to add boiling water during the last period of cooking.

5. Serve immediately, sprinkled with chopped parsley.

BLACK-EYED PEAS

Botanically, black-eyed peas belong to the bean family. These legumes were introduced to America in 1674 by African slaves who carried the seeds with them to the New World.

Often cooked with a ham hock or bacon, black-eyed peas are also delicious when served with cream and black pepper. Fresh black-eyed peas are sometimes dressed with sour cream, dill, caraway seeds, and oregano.

RED BEANS AND RICE

For this recipe, dried beans should be used rather than canned; the beans need long, slow cooking to absorb the flavor of the onions, garlic, and salt pork; canned beans will disintegrate.

Red beans are oval-shaped, smaller than red kidney beans, and darker in color than pinto beans. Dried red kidney beans can be substituted.

Serves 6

1 pound dried red beans
¾ pound salt pork
1 cup thinly sliced scallions, including green tops
1 cup chopped onions
1 tablespoon minced garlic
Tabasco
1 cup long-grain rice (do not use instant rice)

1. Wash the beans in several changes of cold water. Put the beans in a saucepan with cold water to cover. Bring to a boil. Remove from the heat, cover the pan, and let the beans stand for 2 hours.

2. In a large quantity of boiling water, blanch the salt pork for 5 minutes. Drain, dry, and chop.

3. Drain the beans, reserving the liquid in which they soaked. Add enough cold water to this liquid to make 2 cups. Set aside.

4. In a saucepan large enough to hold all the ingredients except the rice, sauté the salt pork until brown and crisp, about 15 minutes. Remove and reserve. Discard all but 3 tablespoons fat and sauté ½ cup of the scallions, all the onions, and the garlic in the remaining fat for 5 to 10 minutes, until the vegetables are soft.

5. Add the beans, the 2 cups of liquid, and a few dashes of Tabasco. Bring to a boil, partially cover the beans, and simmer gently for about 2 hours, adding the reserved salt pork during the last hour. During the last half hour of cooking, if all the liquid is absorbed, add up to 4 tablespoons of boiling water to the pan. Stir frequently, mashing some of the softest beans against the sides of the pan to form a sauce.

6. In a large pot, bring 4 quarts of water to a boil. Pour in the rice and simmer for 12 minutes. Set your timer. Drain in a colander.

7. Put the rice in a bowl, spoon the beans on top, and serve immediately, sprinkled with the remaining ½ cup of scallions.

CORNMEAL AND CHEESE CASSEROLE

Serves 6–8

1 ½ cups cold, cooked cornmeal mush (see page 55)
8 tablespoons (1 stick) unsalted butter
¼ cup chopped green pepper or 2 table-spoons chopped fresh jalapeño or ser-rano chili
¾ cup grated hard cheese (Gruyère, Parme-san, or sharp Cheddar)

1. Preheat the oven to 375° F.

2. Slice the cold mush into pieces ½ inch thick. Cover the bottom of an 8-inch baking dish (or its equivalent) with half the slices. Dot with 4 tablespoons of the butter, sprinkle on the pepper or chili and half the cheese. Cover with remaining cormeal slices, butter, and cheese.

3. Bake for 25 to 30 minutes or until the cheese is melted and browned. Serve immediately.

Vegetables

STEWED CORN AND TOMATOES

Late summer, when corn and tomatoes are plentiful (indeed, often overabundant), is the time to make this delicious combination. It's a flexible recipe; more or less tomato, onion, corn, or pepper is up to you.

Serves 6

4 ears corn
4 strips bacon
1 cup chopped onions
2–3 cups peeled, seeded, and chopped fresh
    tomatoes
½ cup chopped green pepper
Pinch sugar
Salt
Freshly ground black pepper
Tabasco

1. Holding the corn at the narrow end with the wide end in a shallow bowl, cut off the kernels with a knife. Don't attempt to cut all the way to the cob. With the dull end or the side of the knife, scrape what remains on the ear, along with the juice. You should have 2½ to 3 cups of corn kernels.

2. Fry the bacon until crisp. Remove and reserve. In 3 tablespoons of the fat remaining in the skillet, sauté the onions for 10 minutes or until they soften.

3. Add the corn kernels to the skillet and cook 10 minutes more, stirring from time to time.

4. Add the tomatoes, green pepper, sugar, salt, pepper, and a few dashes of Tabasco. Cover the skillet and cook for 25 minutes. Serve sprinkled with the reserved bacon, crumbled.

CORN

Ninety percent of the sugar in sweet corn turns to starch within an hour of picking. People who grow their own corn don't even pick it until the kettle of water is boiling.

Nongrowers should keep the corn unhusked in the refrigerator until they are ready to cook it. To help a little, add sugar to the boiling water and use no salt at all. Salt water toughens kernels even more than prolonged exposure to air.

In the South, some cooks who cannot toss the corn directly from the stalk to the pot cook the cobs in equal amounts of milk and water, enough to cover the cobs; several tablespoons butter are added to the liquid. They cook the corn for 8 to 10 minutes and claim it will keep in the milk-water mixture for at least an hour after the pot is removed from the heat.

Leftover kernels from cooked, fresh corn can be removed from the cob and frozen. Reheat quickly in a little boiling water and toss with butter.

MUSTARD GREENS

Mustard greens are not usually available at your local supermarket, but farm stands, farmers' markets, and your own garden may yield them. If you can find them, they're worth cooking for their tangy taste. Collard or turnip greens or a combination of either or both of them with mustard greens can be prepared in the same way. Collard greens have the toughest texture of the three.

Serves 5–6

4 pounds mustard greens
6 tablespoons diced bacon
½ cup chopped onions
4 tablespoons cider vinegar
Salt
Freshly ground black pepper
Sugar

1. Prepare the greens as you would spinach: discard the stems and tough ribs. (The cleaned weight will be 36 to 40 ounces of greens—those stems and ribs weigh a lot.) Soak the leaves in several changes of cold water.

2. Cook the greens in a large enameled pot, covered, in only the water clinging to the leaves. Cook until tender, about 30 minutes, stirring from time to time. Watch them closely toward the end of cooking time because as the moisture evaporates the greens are more likely to scorch. Add more water, if necessary. The greens will have reduced so dramatically in bulk as to make you wonder why you used such a big pot.

3. Drain the greens and purée them in the container of a blender or food processor, or chop them finely with a sharp knife. You should have about 2 cups.

4. Sauté the bacon. Remove when the pieces are crisp and set them aside on paper towels. In the fat remaining in the skillet, sauté the onions for about 5 minutes. Add the vinegar and greens, salt, pepper, and a pinch of sugar. Heat through and serve sprinkled with the reserved bacon.

TANGY HOT BEETS

Serves 6

6-8 cooked, peeled beets
2 tablespoons unsalted butter
1 teaspoon sugar
1 tablespoon white vinegar
Salt
Freshly ground black pepper
1 tablespoon chopped chervil or parsley

1. Thinly slice the beets, and in a saucepan over low heat, toss them with the butter, sugar, vinegar, salt, and pepper.

2. Just before serving, sprinkle with the chopped herb.

BEETS

Beets are nutritious, versatile, delicious, and, no matter what you combine them with, an absolutely beautiful color.

When buying beets, choose the smallest ones available, no more than roughly 5 inches in circumference. In early summer, choose beets the size of walnuts; they are wonderful.

Beets require a preliminary cooking. Leave about 1½ inches of stem and ½ inch of tail. Wash gently under cold water; don't scrub and try not to pierce the beets. Place on a steamer in a large pot with an inch or two of water in the bottom. Bring to a boil, cover, and steam for 30 to 40 minutes. You may need to add more boiling water to the bottom of the pot. When done, the beets will feel tender to the touch. You can also boil the beets in simmering water to cover in a tightly covered pot for 30 to 60 minutes, depending on size. Or bake the beets in a 325°F. oven for about 1 hour. When the beets are cool enough to handle, slice off the stem and slip off the skins.

HERBED BEETS

Serves 6

6-8 cooked, peeled beets
2 tablespoons unsalted butter
2 tablespoons chopped scallions or shallots
3 tablespoons chopped parsley, chervil, or
    chives

1. Slice or quarter the cooked beets.

2. In a saucepan, over low heat, toss the beets with the butter and scallions or shallots. Serve when hot, sprinkled with one or more of the chopped herbs.

BARBARA'S SAUTEED PEPPERS AND ONIONS

These can be made in advance and reheated just before serving.

Serves 6

3 tablespoons olive oil
3 tablespoons chopped garlic
2–2½ cups chopped onions
2 pounds green or red bell peppers or a combination
Salt
Freshly ground black pepper
2 tablespoons wine vinegar

1. In a heavy 10–inch skillet over very low heat, sauté the garlic in the olive oil for 5 or 6 minutes, stirring often. Don't let the garlic brown.

2. Add the onions to the skillet and cook slowly for 15 to 20 minutes. Slow cooking develops the onions' sweetness.

3. Wash and seed the peppers. Cut them into strips approximately ½ inch wide and 2 inches long, discarding the white ribs.

4. Add the peppers to the skillet and cook 15 to 20 minutes. The peppers should retain their crunchy texture. Season with salt and pepper.

5. Add the wine vinegar; raise the heat to boil off most of the vinegar. Serve immediately, or set aside uncovered and reheat gently before serving.

BUTTERED TURNIPS

Serves 4–6

2 pounds small turnips
2 tablespoons unsalted butter
1 tablespoon chopped parsley and/or chives
Salt
Freshly ground black pepper

1. Peel the turnips and cut them into julienne strips or thin rounds or slices. Cook them in an inch or two of boiling salted water for 5 minutes or until barely tender.

2. Drain the turnips, put them back in the warm pot, and toss with butter, herbs, salt, and pepper. Serve immediately.

MASHED TURNIPS. Cook the turnips about 8 minutes or until fully tender. Mash with a fork or put through a food mill and combine with 3 tablespoons unsalted butter and 3 tablespoons heavy cream. Season with salt and pepper, and sprinkle with 1 tablespoon minced parsley.

TURNIPS AND BACON

Serves 4–6

2 pounds small turnips
¼ cup diced bacon
½ cup chopped onions
Salt
Freshly ground black pepper
2 tablespoons minced parsley

1. Peel and thinly slice the turnips. Cook in boiling salted water to cover for 5 minutes. Drain and set aside.

2. Sauté the bacon in a heavy skillet until crisp. Add the onions and cook until soft and golden, 7 to 10 minutes over low heat.

3. Add the turnips, cook about 10 minutes. Serve immediately, seasoned with salt and pepper and sprinkled with parsley.

TURNIPS

Turnips are a root vegetable belonging to the cabbage family. They have long been cultivated in America. In 1540, Carter sowed turnips seeds during his third voyage. Buy the smallest turnips you can find. They should be firm with unblemished skins. Turnips have a delicious nutlike flavor, and they deserve to be eaten on their own, not just disguised in stews.

BAKED ONIONS

Easy and delicious, these onions take only 5 minutes to prepare and require no attention at all during the cooking. The slow cooking from the heat of the charcoal makes them soft and sweet. They are also good cooked for 1 hour in a 350° F. oven.

Serves 6

6 large white onions
6 teaspoons unsalted butter (2 tablespoons)

1. Peel the onions and cut a deep cross in the stem end.

2. Place a teaspoon of butter over the cuts and wrap each onion in a triple thickness of aluminum foil.

3. Place the onions around the perimeter of the hot coals and leave undisturbed for 1 ½ to 2 hours. Unwrap and serve.

EMBER COOKING

Some vegetables are really wonderful when buried directly in the coals.

Potatoes: Rub the skins lightly with oil and wrap the potatoes in a double thickness of aluminum foil. Cook until soft when pierced, about an hour, turning occasionally.

Squash: Butternut or acorn squash can be cooked unwrapped in the hot coals. Cook for 45 to 60 minutes. Cut open, remove seeds, and serve with butter and brown sugar.

Corn: Soak the corn, silk and husk included, in ice water for 30 minutes. Shake off excess water and roast directly in the coals, wrapped in foil or not, for 30 to 45 minutes, turning often. Serve with butter.

FRIED ONION RINGS

I immodestly proclaim these to be the best fried onion rings I've ever eaten. On the down side, you feel like a short-order cook while preparing them. As soon as a batch is done, serve it and keep your fingers crossed that there will be some left by the time you get to the table.

Serves 6

3 pounds onions (buy large onions so the
     rings will be large)
1 cup water
1 cup flour
Vegetable oil
Salt

1. Slice the onions about ¼ inch thick, break them into rings, and place in a large bowl. Cover with cold water and ice cubes. Soak for 2 hours.

2. Put the cup of water in a bowl and slowly beat in the flour. The batter should have the consistency of thick buttermilk.

3. Heat ¾ inch of oil in a large, heavy skillet.

4. Drain the onion rings and dip them in the batter.

5. Fry them in the hot oil, making sure you don't crowd the pan. When the onion rings are golden brown, drain on paper towels, salt, and serve.

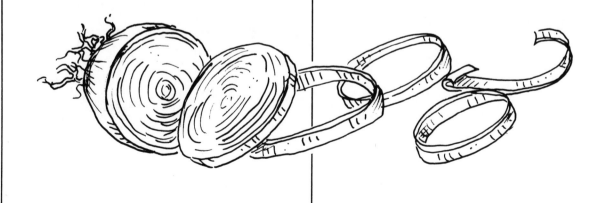

FRIED OKRA

Buy small fresh or frozen baby okra for this recipe. Defrost frozen okra as described in the recipe for Corn and Okra Creole (page 69).

Serves 6

2 pounds fresh baby okra or 2 10-ounce packages frozen baby okra
1 cup white or yellow cornmeal
Salt
Freshly ground black pepper
Vegetable oil

1. Wash and slice the okra into rounds ¼ to ½ inch thick.

2. Put the cornmeal, seasoned with salt and pepper, into a brown paper bag. Add the okra slices and shake vigorously.

3. Heat ¾ inch of oil in a large heavy skillet. Remove okra slices from the paper bag with a slotted spoon and fry, turning and tossing constantly, until golden, 3 or 4 minutes. Don't crowd the skillet and add more oil as necessary. Drain the okra slices on paper towels and serve immediately.

OKRA

Okra, a tapered green pod that grows up to nine inches long, has been prized in Africa since prehistoric times. Like black-eyed peas, okra was brought to America by slaves who called it gumbo—a name later extended to the stew that is thickened by the gummy substance in the okra pod.

CORN AND OKRA CREOLE

If you use frozen okra, defrost it in a bowl of cold water or under running cold tap water until the pieces can be separated. Dry as thoroughly as you can in several layers and changes of paper towels. Frozen corn should be handled the same way.

Serves 6

1 ½ cups chopped green pepper
1 cup sliced onions
4 tablespoons lard or unsalted butter
1 ½ cups fresh corn kernels (2–4 ears), or 1
    10-ounce package frozen corn
1 pound small fresh baby okra, sliced, or 1
    10-ounce package frozen okra
1 20-ounce can whole, peeled tomatoes,
    drained and chopped
¼ teaspoon thyme
Cayenne
Salt
Sugar
Freshly ground black pepper
1 teaspoon strong mustard

1. In a large, heavy skillet, sauté the green pepper and onions in the lard or butter for 15 or 20 minutes, stirring often. Add the corn and okra and cook for 10 minutes more, stirring.

2. Add the tomatoes, thyme, a pinch each of cayenne and sugar, salt and pepper to taste. Finally, add the mustard. Stir, cover, and cook over low heat for 30 minutes.

CORN FRITTERS

These fritters are light and delicious and can be made with fresh corn, canned corn, or kernels removed from leftover cooked corn. They are a short-order item and the batter should be made just before frying; but from start to finish, these fritters take no more than 15 minutes to prepare.

Makes about 20 2– to 2½ -inch fritters; serves 6

4 eggs, separated
4 tablespoons all-purpose flour
½ teaspoon baking powder
Salt
Freshly ground black pepper
Nutmeg
2 cups fresh corn kernels (from 3–5 ears), or
    2 scant cups canned whole kernel corn (1
    17-ounce can)
Butter and vegetable oil for frying

1. Beat the egg yolks until paler. Beating and mashing with a wooden spoon, add the flour, baking powder, salt and pepper to taste, a few gratings of nutmeg, and the corn, drained if you are using canned.

2. Beat the egg whites until stiff but not dry. Fold them into the batter.

3. In a large heavy skillet heat to just smoking enough butter and oil to reach a depth of ¼ inch. Drop the batter by tablespoonsful into the skillet and cook until golden brown, about 4 minutes on each side. Regulate the heat so the fat doesn't burn, and don't crowd the pan. It will be necessary to add more butter and oil to the skillet during the frying. Drain on paper towels; serve immediately.

CREAMED SPINACH

This is an untraditional but excellent accompaniment to ribs: it tastes delicious and is a mild foil for spicy ribs.

Serves 4–6

2 10-ounce packages frozen chopped spinach
Salt
½ teaspoon baking soda
2 tablespoons unsalted butter
1 tablespoon flour
½ cup heavy cream, chicken stock, or beef
    broth

1. Put the spinach in an enameled pan. Sprinkle with salt, cover, and place over low heat. From time to time, uncover and break up what you can with a wooden spoon. When the spinach has defrosted, in approximately 15 minutes, raise the heat to evaporate the moisture, stirring so the spinach doesn't scorch. Add the baking soda and butter, stirring until the butter melts.

2. Add the flour and cook, stirring, for 3 to 4 minutes.

3. Pour in the cream or stock, cover, and cook slowly for 10 minutes, adding more liquid by the spoonful, if necessary. If not to be served immediately, leave uncovered. Reheat with 1 or 2 more tablespoons liquid.

Salads

MIRIAM WEBER'S COLE SLAW

Caraway seeds or toasted ground cumin seeds are a good addition to this recipe.

Serves 6

1 1½-pound cabbage
Kosher salt
1 carrot
¼ green pepper
1 celery stalk
4 tablespoons mayonnaise
1 tablespoon fresh lemon juice
½ tablespoon sugar

1. Quarter, core, and shred the cabbage. Place in a colander, sprinkle generously with salt, and let stand for 15 to 30 minutes.

2. Shred the carrot on a coarse grater; cut the green pepper into 1-inch strips and slice the strips crosswise into ¼-inch pieces. Cut celery into similar-size pieces. Combine the three vegetables.

3. Combine 2 tablespoons of the mayonnaise, the lemon juice, and sugar. Beat until well mixed.

4. With the remaining 2 tablespoons mayonnaise, smear the bottom and sides of your serving bowl.

5. Wash the cabbage in cold water and drain thoroughly. Pat dry with paper towels.

6. Place a layer of the drained cabbage in the bottom of the bowl, cover with mixed vegetables and a thin layer of the mayonnaise mixture. When all has been added, mix thoroughly and taste. You may need more mayonnaise or lemon juice.

CABBAGE

Cabbage is so rich in minerals and vitamins, C in particular, that it has been called man's best friend in the vegetable kingdom.

Aristotle was said to have followed the Egyptian practice of eating cabbage before a banquet, thinking it would keep the wine from fogging his brain.

CREAMY COLE SLAW

Serves 6–8

1 2- to 3-pound cabbage
1 cup sour cream
3 tablespoons tarragon vinegar
1 teaspoon dry mustard
½ cup mayonnaise
1 teaspoon toasted ground cumin seeds (see
    page 22)

1. Remove the coarse outer leaves of the cabbage. Halve, remove the core, and shred the cabbage, either by hand with a sharp knife making ⅛-inch-wide slices or with the slicing (*not* the shredding) disc of a food processor.

2. Soak the cabbage in ice water to cover for at least 1 hour; this will yield a very crisp cole slaw.

3. In a large bowl in which you plan to serve the cole slaw, combine the remaining ingredients. Mix well with a wire whisk or fork.

4. Just before serving, drain the cabbage. Pat as dry as possible with paper towels and combine with the dressing, mixing well.

COLE SLAW

As new settlers arrived in America from European countries, they introduced from their native lands foods adapted to indigenous ingredients. The Dutch brought *kool sla*, cabbage salad, which has become, of course, cole slaw.

Buy firm, young cabbage with compact leaves. Cabbage with floppy outer leaves is old and lacks moisture and taste. The outer leaves, removed before you shred the cabbage, can be used to line the dish in which you serve the slaw.

Shredded cabbage looks better and seems to taste better than chopped cabbage. The slicing disc of a food processor will shred a cabbage in seconds. To shred by hand, use a long, thin, sharp knife. Cut the cabbage in half, remove the core, and place the cabbage cut-side down on a chopping board. Slice across in thin strips.

The use of salt has a lot (virtually all) to do with the texture of the cole slaw. Salt will wilt the cabbage almost instantly because it releases the water in the cabbage. Preliminary soaking in ice water for at least an hour will keep cabbage crunchy after you've dressed it, though only for a few hours; leftovers will be wilted—good, but texturally different.

Cole slaw can be varied almost endlessly, and you should experiment. Try dressings made of yogurt and cider vinegar; add *crème fraîche* or heavy cream; try walnut oil or sesame oil. (Oriental sesame oil is quite strong so, to start, add just a teaspoon or two to your dressing.) Experiment with various herbs and spices: dill, chives, chervil, hot red pepper flakes, cayenne, celery or caraway seeds.

GALE'S COLE SLAW

Serves 6–8

1 2- to 3-pound cabbage
2 carrots
½ onion
1 cup mayonnaise
1 tablespoon white vinegar
Juice of ½ lemon
2 scallions, chopped
Salt
Freshly ground black pepper

1. Remove the coarse outer leaves of the cabbage, halve, and remove the core. Either by hand with a sharp knife or in a processor fitted with the slicing disc (*not* the shredding disc), shred the cabbage.

2. Grate the carrots and onion (these should have a finer consistency than the cabbage, so using the shredding disc is fine). Combine the grated vegetables with the cabbage.

3. In a large bowl in which you plan to serve the cole slaw, combine the remaining ingredients. Mix well.

4. Just before serving, toss the dressing and the vegetables together.

RED CABBAGE AND APPLE SLAW

Serves 6

3 tablespoons wine vinegar
8 tablespoons olive oil
1 teaspoon dry mustard
1 tablespoon minced shallot
1 teaspoon prepared white horseradish
1 1-pound red cabbage
3 large, firm apples, peeled and cored
Salt
Freshly ground black pepper

1. In a large serving bowl, make a dressing with the wine vinegar, olive oil, mustard, shallot, and horseradish. Mix well with a wire whisk.

2. In a food processor fitted with the slicing disc, shred the cabbage and apples. This can also be done by hand, making ⅛-inch-wide slices with a long, sharp knife.

3. Combine the cabbage and apples with the dressing. Toss well and let stand for 3 or 4 hours. Add salt and pepper before serving.

BACON POTATO SALAD

Serves 6

3 pounds small red potatoes (buy potatoes of
    uniform size so they will be done at the
    same time)
½ pound bacon, chopped
1 cup chopped onions
2 tablespoons wine vinegar
1 tablespoon white vinegar
5 tablespoons olive oil
Salt
Freshly ground black pepper
1 cup chopped scallions, including green tops
½ cup chopped parsley

1. Scrub the potatoes and place them in a large pan of cold water to cover. Bring to a boil, lower heat, and cook until the potatoes are just done, about 15 minutes after the water comes to a boil.

2. While the potatoes are boiling, fry the bacon pieces in a small, heavy skillet (a 6- or 7-inch cast-iron one is good). When done, drain on paper towels and pour off all but 4 tablespoons of the bacon fat. In the bacon fat remaining in the skillet, fry the onions just until they wilt.

3. When the potatoes are done, drain them. Using paper towels or potholders to handle the hot potatoes, quarter them directly into the serving bowl.

4. Pour the onions, bacon, and cooking fat over the potatoes.

5. Add the vinegars, olive oil, salt, and pepper. Toss gently with a wooden spoon. When the salad cools, add the scallions and parsley.

6. Taste before serving; the salad may need more olive oil and/or vinegar, as well as more salt and pepper.

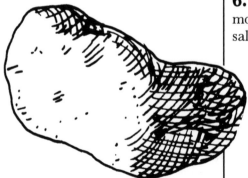

CREAMY BEET SALAD

Both this salad and the Beets Vinaigrette, which follows, are good with the addition of chopped hard-boiled eggs and/or cold cooked vegetables such as green beans or zucchini.

Serves 6–8

7–8 medium beets, cooked and peeled (see page 63)
¼ cup sour cream
½ teaspoon prepared white horseradish
½ teaspoon Dijon mustard
2 tablespoons mayonnaise
2 tablespoons chopped chives, parsley, or dill

1. Slice, dice, or chop the beets.

2. Combine the remaining ingredients except the herbs in the bowl in which you plan to serve the beets. Add the beets and mix gently but well. Refrigerate for 1 to 2 hours. Before serving, sprinkle with one or more of the chopped herbs.

BEETS VINAIGRETTE

Serves 6–8

7–8 medium beets, cooked and peeled (see page 63)
1 tablespoon wine vinegar
¼ teaspoon dry mustard
4 tablespoons olive oil
2 tablespoons minced shallots or scallions
2 tablespoons chopped parsley and/or chives

1. Slice, chop, or dice the beets.

2. Combine the vinegar, mustard, oil, and shallots or scallions in a screw-top jar and shake vigorously.

3. Pour the vinaigrette over the beets, mix well, sprinkle with chopped herbs, and serve.

CARROT SALAD

Serves 6–8

2 bunches carrots (about 1 ½ –2 pounds)
1 cup chopped onions or scallions (with green tops) or a combination of both
3 tablespoons fresh lemon juice
7 tablespoons olive oil
¼ teaspoon dry mustard
Salt
Freshly ground black pepper
2 tablespoons (or more) chopped chives or parsley

1. Scrape the carrots and shred in a food processor or standing electric mixer with a shredder attachment.

2. In a large serving bowl, combine the lemon juice, olive oil, mustard, salt, and pepper. Add the carrots and mix well.

3. Let stand for at least 30 minutes before serving, sprinkled with the chives or parsley.

CARROT AND TURNIP SALAD

The sharp nuttiness of the raw turnips combined with the sweetness of the carrots is unexpectedly delicious as well as very pretty.

Serves 6–8

1 pound small turnips
1 pound carrots
4 tablespoons fresh lemon juice
½ cup olive oil

6 tablespoons snipped dill or minced parsley
Salt
Freshly ground black pepper

1. Peel the turnips and carrots and shred or grate them in a food processor.

2. Transfer to a serving bowl and add the remaining ingredients. Toss well to combine. Serve immediately or let stand for several hours. The vegetables will soften as they sit in the dressing.

RICE SALAD

This basic rice salad recipe can be varied according to taste and what you have on hand. Leftover chicken, shrimp, or beef make it a rather substantial dish; strips of pimiento add color; barely cooked peas or green beans add texture.

Serves 6

1 cup long-grain rice (do not use instant rice)
½ cup chopped onions or scallions
1 teaspoon dried tarragon
4 tablespoons white vinegar
6 tablespoons olive oil
Salt
Freshly ground black pepper
½ cup (or more) minced parsley, tarragon, and/or chives

1. In at least 4 quarts of salted, rapidly boiling water, cook the rice for exactly 12 minutes. If you use too little water the rice will be gummy; if you cook it too long the rice will be mushy.

2. Drain the rice well, shaking the colander and tossing the rice with a wooden spoon to remove as much moisture as possible.

3. Transfer the rice to a large serving bowl and immediately toss with the onions or scallions, dried tarragon, vinegar, olive oil, salt, and pepper. Any meat or vegetables you include should be added at this point. Set aside to cool.

4. Before serving, toss with one or more of the fresh herbs. Taste carefully: more olive oil, vinegar, salt, or pepper might be needed. Refrigerated, the rice salad will keep for several days. Bring to room temperature before serving.

RICE

America's cultivation of rice began shortly after 1694. According to one legend, a ship from Madagascar was thrown off course and its captain and crew received hospitality in Charleston. Landgrave T. Smith, a settler, obtained rice seeds from the ship's captain. Smith planted the seeds in the governor's garden and the whole Carolina colony was supplied by the first harvest.

CHICK PEA AND GREEN BEAN SALAD

Serves 6

1 tablespoon fresh lemon juice
1 tablespoon wine vinegar
2 teaspoons chopped garlic
Salt
Freshly ground black pepper
Cayenne
1 tablespoon grated fresh ginger
1 teaspoon toasted ground cumin seeds (see
     page 22)
¼ cup chopped scallions, including green
     tops
½ cup olive oil
1 pound green beans, trimmed
1 1-pound can chick peas
2 ripe tomatoes (optional)

TRIMMING AND COOKING GREEN BEANS

To trim beans, snap off the ends and pull down to remove any strings. Nowadays, most beans seem not to have strings, but some do and they are unpleasant to eat.

Bring a large quantity of *unsalted* water to a boil. Add the beans. Add salt when the water returns to the boil. Salting at this time sets the green color. No matter how they are ultimately served, the beans should have a crunchy texture. Boil for no more than 5 minutes and then run under cold water or plunge them into ice water to stop them from further cooking.

1. Make a dressing in the bowl in which you plan to serve the salad. Place the lemon juice and wine vinegar in the bowl. Add the garlic, salt, pepper, a pinch of cayenne, ginger, cumin seeds, and scallions. Beat with a wire whisk to combine. Slowly beat in the olive oil.

2. Blanch the beans in a large quantity of boiling water for 2 minutes. Drain, run under cold water, and pat dry with paper towels. Cut the beans into 2-inch lengths and toss with the dressing.

3. Put the chick peas in a colander and rinse under cold running water to remove the taste of the canning juices. Pat dry and add to the dressing. Toss gently but well.

4. Let stand for 2 or 3 hours or up to 6 hours in the refrigerator before serving. If you refrigerate the salad, bring it to room temperature before serving. Garnish with optional tomato wedges.

CORN SALAD

This salad is best served 2 to 3 hours after it is prepared. The corn exudes a milky liquid and the salad becomes soggy after 12 hours.

Serves 6

6 ears corn
½ cup chopped onions
1 cup chopped celery
½ cup julienned pimiento
6½ tablespoons olive oil
1½ tablespoons wine vinegar
½ teaspoon Dijon mustard
Salt
Freshly ground black pepper
½ cup chopped parsley

1. Boil the corn, covered, in a large kettle of water for 4 to 8 minutes (depending on the age of the corn). When cool enough to handle, remove the kernels with a sharp knife, holding the ear straight up in a bowl and slicing downward.

2. In a serving bowl, combine the corn kernels with the onions, celery, and pimiento.

3. In a screw-top jar or in a small bowl with a wire whisk, combine the oil, vinegar, and mustard. Pour the dressing over the salad and mix.

4. Chill for 2 or 3 hours. Just before serving, add salt, pepper, and parsley. Mix gently but well.

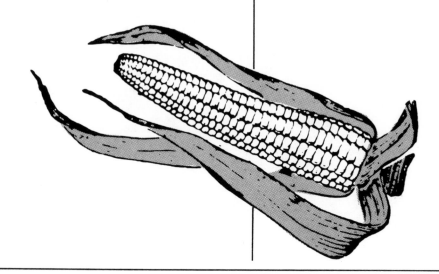

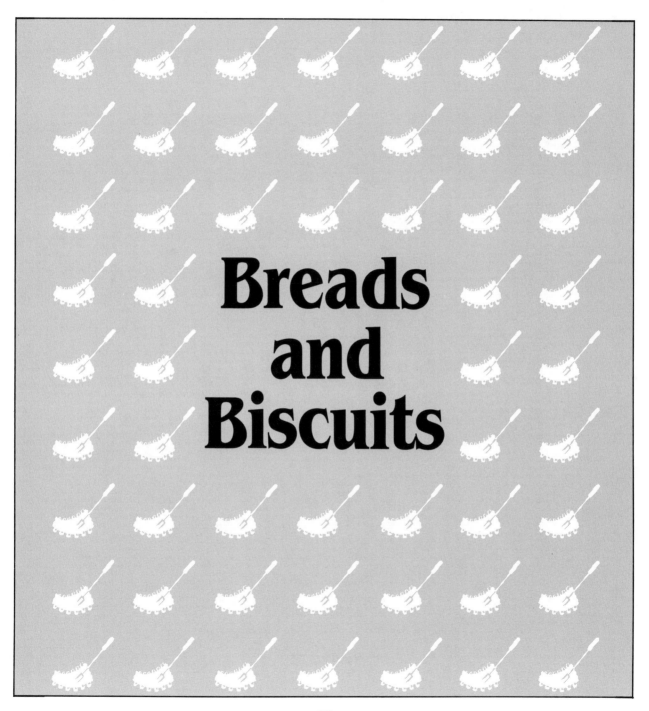

Breads and Biscuits

BEATEN BISCUITS

These old-fashioned biscuits are delicious but time-consuming to prepare. Traditionally, the dough is beaten with a mallet or rolling pin for 30 minutes to an hour ("from three to five hundred licks"). If you have a beaten-biscuit machine among your family heirlooms, by all means use it. These machines work like pasta machines with two big rollers pounding and flattening the dough. They are available almost solely through inheritance. A third alternative, and the easiest method, is to put the dough through a meat grinder.

Makes approximately 12 biscuits

1 tablespoon unsalted butter, softened
2 cups all-purpose flour
½ teaspoon salt
1½ teaspoons sugar
½ teaspoon baking powder
3 tablespoons (1½ ounces) lard
¼ cup milk combined with ¼ cup water

1. Preheat the oven to 350° F.

2. Butter a large cookie sheet and set aside.

3. Combine the flour, salt, sugar, and baking powder. Cut in the lard. Work the dough with your fingertips or the dough arm of a standing electric mixer until it looks mealy.

4. Add the liquid, a little at a time, rubbing and kneading after each addition. Knead the dough until it is smooth.

5. Place the dough on a flat surface and beat with a mallet or rolling pin. You needn't strike the dough with great force, only hard enough to flatten it to a thickness of about ½ inch. As you beat, fold the dough over on itself frequently, whenever it is flattened to ½ inch, beating and folding anywhere from 30 to 45 minutes. (The traditional "five hundred licks" take only 6 or 7 minutes.) The longer you beat the more blistered, shiny, and elastic the dough will become.

Alternatively, put the dough, over and over, for 20 to 30 minutes through the rollers of the beaten-biscuit machine.

Finally (and easiest), you can put the dough through the coarsest blade of a meat grinder four times. The dough must be elastic and satiny.

6. Roll the dough to a thickness of ¼ inch and cut into 2-inch rounds using a biscuit cutter or the rim of a demitasse cup.

7. Place the biscuits, about an inch apart, on the buttered cookie sheet. Prick the tops with the tines of a fork and bake for 25 minutes or until the biscuits are lightly browned. Serve immediately with butter.

BUTTERMILK BISCUITS

Buttermilk biscuits have a distinctive flavor and a tender texture.

Makes 1 dozen

2 cups all-purpose flour
1 teaspoon salt
1 tablespoon baking powder
1 teaspoon baking soda
4 tablespoons unsalted butter or vegetable shortening
¾ cup buttermilk
3 tablespoons unsalted butter, melted

1. Preheat the oven to 450° F.

2. Combine the dry ingredients and sift them together into a bowl.

3. Cut in the butter or shortening and mix with your fingertips, 2 forks, or a pastry blender until the mixture is crumbly.

4. Stir in the buttermilk and blend only until the batter holds together.

5. Turn the dough onto a floured surface and knead for 2 or 3 minutes.

6. Roll the dough, using light pressure, into a circle about ½ inch thick.

7. Using a cookie cutter or the rim of a glass, cut the dough into circles 2 to 3 inches in diameter. Place on an ungreased baking sheet and paint the top of each biscuit with melted butter.

8. Bake for 8 to 10 minutes or until tops are golden.

CORN BREAD

This corn bread recipe is very versatile. With the addition of bacon, salt pork, or crackling (if you've rendered your own pork fat) it becomes crackling bread; baked in a corn-stick pan, you have, naturally, corn sticks; when baked in a cast-iron skillet the same batter becomes skillet or spider corn bread (the spider is an old-fashioned iron skillet with three feet, which was set in the fireplace directly over the hot coals).

Makes 14–16 corn sticks or 1 bread, to serve 6

2 tablespoons (1 ounce) lard
1½ cups cornmeal (water- or stone-ground white cornmeal yields the lightest bread; but commercially ground yellow cornmeal is acceptable)
½ cup all-purpose flour
1½ teaspoons salt
½ teaspoon baking soda
1 tablespoon baking powder
2 eggs, lightly beaten
2 cups buttermilk

1. Preheat the oven to 400° F.

2. Put the lard in a 9- or 10-inch cast-iron skillet or divide it among the 7 or 8 compartments of a corn-stick mold and place the prepared pan in the oven.

3. Combine the dry ingredients in a large bowl.

4. Add the eggs and the buttermilk. Stir well, removing any lumps with the backs of 2 wooden spoons.

5. Remove the skillet or mold from the oven and tilt it so that all the surfaces are well greased. Pour the excess lard into the batter and stir.

6. Pour the batter into the hot pan and bake, at 400° F., for 25 to 30 minutes. The bread should have golden brown edges, the top will be dotted with golden brown patches, and the bread should test clean.

CORN STICKS. Fill the mold ¾ full and bake for 15 to 20 minutes. Regrease the mold and fill with the remaining batter.

CRACKLING BREAD. Instead of using lard in step 2, sauté ½ pound diced (1 cup) bacon or diced salt pork in a 9- or 10-inch cast-iron skillet. Remove the crisp bits and tilt the pan so that its surface is coated with the fat. Pour 2 or 3 tablespoons of the bacon fat and the bacon bits into the batter in step 5. Reduce the amount of salt to ½ teaspoon.

JALAPEÑO CORN BREAD. Add a diced fresh jalapeño pepper to the dry ingredients in step 3.

SPOON BREAD

Spoon bread is more like a pudding than a bread and may have its origins in the Indian cornmeal-and-water porridge called *sappawn*.

Serves 6

4½ tablespoons unsalted butter
2⅔ cups milk
1 cup cornmeal (white or yellow, preferably stone- or water-ground)
3 eggs, lightly beaten
⅓ cup sour cream, at room temperature
1½ teaspoons baking powder
½ teaspoon baking soda
Pinch of salt

1. Preheat the oven to 400° F.

2. Using 1 tablespoon of the butter, grease a 1½-quart baking dish and set aside.

3. Heat the milk in a large, heavy saucepan. When bubbles form around the edges, pour in the cornmeal in a slow, steady stream, stirring constantly with a wooden spoon. Alternatively, shake the cornmeal through a sieve directly into the milk. With the backs of 2 wooden spoons, break up any lumps as they form.

4. Off the heat, stir the eggs slowly into the cornmeal, beating vigorously with the wooden spoon as you do so.

5. Add the remaining butter, a teaspoon at a time, stirring until it melts. Add the sour cream.

6. Finally add the baking powder, baking soda, and salt. Stir the batter and pour into the buttered baking dish.

7. Bake in the preheated oven for 45 minutes, or until firm and brown on top.

8. Serve the bread immediately, right from the baking dish, with plenty of butter.

CHEDDAR SPOON BREAD. Add a pinch of cayenne and 1 cup (4 ounces) grated sharp Cheddar cheese just before adding the baking powder in step 6.

CORNMEAL

In a letter to the *Gazetteer*, a London newspaper, Benjamin Franklin, signing himself "Homespun," wrote a passionate defense of corn. It was during the dispute over the Stamp Act and was published on January 2, 1766.

Vindex Patriae, a writer in your paper, comforts himself, and the India Company, with the fancy, that the Americans, should they resolve to drink no more tea, can by no means keep that resolution, their Indian corn not affording "an agreeable or easy digestible breakfast." Pray let me, an American, inform the gentleman, who seems ignorant of the matter, that Indian corn, take it for all in all, is one of the most agreeable and wholesome grains in the world. . . . and the johnny or hoecake, hot from the fire, is better than a Yorkshire muffin . . . .

SALLY LUNN

This yeast bread originated in England and may have been named for the woman who popularized it. William Makepeace Thackeray described a meal of "green tea, scandal, hot Sally Lunns, and a little novel reading."

Yields 1 high 10-inch loaf

1 package (¼ ounce) dry active yeast
¼ cup sugar
¼ cup warm water (100°–110° F.)
¾ cup warm milk (100°–110° F.)
8 tablespoons (1 stick) unsalted butter,
    melted in the milk
1 teaspoon salt
3 eggs, lightly beaten
3½–4 cups all-purpose flour

1. In a mixing bowl or the bowl of a standing electric mixer fitted with a dough hook, sprinkle the yeast and sugar over the warm water. Let stand for 5 minutes, then stir the ingredients and leave the mixture to proof.

2. Stir the milk, butter, salt, and eggs into the yeast mixture.

3. Add the flour, ½ cup at a time, beating thoroughly with a wooden spoon after each addition. If you use a standing mixer, you'll have to stop the machine from time to time to incorporate the flour sticking to the sides of the bowl. The dough should be stiff but workable.

4. Cover the bowl and let the dough rise slowly in a cool place until double in bulk. (This should take 1½–2 hours; but kitchen conditions and yeast are variable.)

5. Punch down the dough and with your hand or a wooden spoon beat, don't knead, for about 1 minute.

6. Transfer the mixture, creating as even a top as you can, to a well-buttered 9- or 10-inch tube pan, kugelhopf, or turk's-head pan. Let the batter rise again—this time to the top of the pan.

7. Preheat the oven to 375° F.

8. Bake the bread in the preheated oven for 40 to 50 minutes or until golden brown. A skewer or toothpick inserted into the bread should come out clean.

9. Cool on a rack and serve warm or at room temperature with butter or jam. Any leftovers should be frozen; sliced and toasted or used for French toast, Sally Lunn is very good.

SALLY LUNN BUNS. Pour the batter into well-greased muffin tins, filling them halfway. Cover with a clean towel, let rise to the top of the muffin tins. Brush with beaten egg mixed with water, and bake at 375° F. for 15 to 20 minutes.

Pickles, Relishes, and Chutneys

BREAD AND BUTTER PICKLES

Makes about 2 quarts

4 pounds unwaxed cucumbers
1 pound onions, thinly sliced
½ cup kosher salt
4 garlic cloves
2½ cups sugar
1½ teaspoons turmeric
1½ teaspoons celery seeds
2 teaspoons mustard seeds
3 cups cider vinegar

1. Slice the unpeeled cucumbers ⅛ inch thick, discarding any soft or rotten spots. Place the cucumber slices, the sliced onions, the salt, and the whole, peeled garlic cloves in a glass or enameled bowl or pot. Add water to cover along with a tray of ice cubes. Cover and refrigerate for 3 or 4 hours or overnight. Drain well, rinse in cold water, and drain again. Place in a colander set over a bowl while you continue with the recipe.

2. In a 6- to 8-quart saucepan, combine the sugar, spices, and vinegar. Bring to a boil, stirring to dissolve the sugar. Add the drained vegetables and heat to a boil.

3. Keeping the mixture below a boil, transfer the pickles to hot sterilized pint jars with a slotted spoon. Fill the jars to 1 inch of their tops.

4. Boil the syrup and pour over the pickles, going to the very tops of the jars. Divide the spices left in the pan among the jars. Any leftover syrup should be discarded. Cover the jars with their lids, cool, and refrigerate. These pickles will get better with time; if you can resist, wait 4 to 6 weeks before eating them.

WATERMELON-RIND PICKLES

As a thrifty cook, I'm delighted to make pickles out of the part of the watermelon that weighs the most and is mainly responsible for the cost, modest as that may be.

You will need about three times the weight in melon that you want in unpeeled rind. Two pounds of parboiled rind will yield about 5 cups of pickled rind.

1 large watermelon
Uniodized or pickling salt
Alum (available at drugstores)
Sugar
White vinegar
Oil of cinnamon or cinnamon stick
Oil of cloves or whole cloves
Lemon
Chopped preserved ginger (optional)

1. Halve the watermelon and scoop out the flesh. Remove the hard green outer skin and scrape off all the remaining pink flesh. Cut the rind into strips and then into ½-inch cubes. Measure the cubes.

2. For every 4 cups of rind, make a brine of 3 tablespoons salt dissolved in 6 cups water. For each gallon of water, add 1 teaspoon alum (to keep the pickles crisp). In a nonaluminum pot, put the rind to soak in the brine. Make sure the rind is completely covered. Weight the rind with a plate and a few cans and refrigerate overnight.

3. Drain the rind and rinse thoroughly in several changes of cold water. Parboil the drained rind in water to cover for about 10 minutes. Drain and measure. For every 8 cups of parboiled rind make a syrup of 4 cups (2 pounds) sugar, 3 cups vinegar, ⅛ teaspoon of the spice oils poured directly into the liquid or 1 teaspoon whole cloves and 1 broken 4-inch cinnamon stick tied together in washed cheesecloth, 3 or 4 thin slices pitted lemon slices. Boil mixture 10 minutes.

4. Add the rind to the syrup and simmer gently for 30 minutes. Remove from the heat, weight the rind as you did when it soaked in the brine, and let stand for 12 to 24 hours.

5. Remove the cheesecloth and bring the rind and syrup to a gentle boil. When thoroughly heated transfer the cubes of rind with a slotted spoon to hot, sterilized jars to within ½ inch of their tops. Boil the syrup and pour over the pickles, making sure they are completely covered. Insert the handle of a long wooden spoon into each jar, pressing against the pickles to release any air bubbles. If you're using it, add a bit of chopped ginger to each jar and put the lids on. Let pickles sit a week or so before serving, well chilled.

CORN RELISH

Makes about 5 cups

4 cups corn kernels (6–8 ears), or 2 packages
    frozen corn
3 cups shredded cabbage (½ pound)
1 cup chopped celery
1 cup chopped red or green bell pepper, or a
    combination
½ cup white vinegar
Scant ¼ cup sugar
1 tablespoon dry mustard
1 tablespoon salt

1. In a large saucepan simmer the corn in ½ cup of water for 3 minutes, until barely tender. Drain and transfer to a large bowl.

2. Place the cabbage, celery, and pepper in a saucepan along with 1 cup water. Bring to a boil, reduce heat, and simmer, covered, for 3 minutes. Drain the vegetables and transfer to the bowl with the corn.

3. In the same saucepan, combine the vinegar, sugar, dry mustard, and salt. Boil for 5 minutes and pour over the vegetables. Mix thoroughly and cool. Transfer to glass jars and refrigerate. It will keep well for several weeks.

TOMATO RELISH

Yields about 3 cups

1 28-ounce can whole tomatoes
2 cups sliced onions
1½ cups sugar
2 cups cider vinegar
½ teaspoon ground cinnamon
½ teaspoon ground allspice
½ teaspoon ground cloves
1 head garlic, cloves peeled and chopped
2 tablespoons grated fresh ginger
2 teaspoons salt
Pinch of cayenne

1. Place all the ingredients, including ½ the juice from the can of tomatoes, in a heavy, 4-quart enameled saucepan. Bring to a boil, lower heat, and simmer gently over low heat for about 1½ hours. As the mixture thickens, stir it from time to time.

2. Let the relish cool before transferring it to a glass jar. It will store covered and refrigerated for several months.

CHILI JAM

This is based on Jane Butel's recipe for red chile jam.

Makes 3 cups

12 large fresh chilies, red or green or a combination
2 small lemons, quartered
½ cup cider vinegar
3 cups sugar

1. Remove seeds from chilies and chop finely (see page 31), or process in a blender or food processor. Use only several on-off motions of the machine so the peppers retain some texture and aren't puréed. You should have 2 cups.

2. In a heavy saucepan, combine the chilies with the lemons and vinegar. Cook for 30 minutes, partially covered. Remove lemon quarters and add sugar.

3. Boil for 10 minutes, or until jam reaches 9 ° F. above boiling. Let the jam cool before transferring to a glass jar and refrigerating. Covered, in the refrigerator, the jam will keep for several months.

FRUIT CHUTNEY

Makes 3 cups

2 tablespoons mixed whole pickling spices, or make your own using cinnamon, allspice, mustard seed, coriander seed, bay leaves, ginger, whole cloves, black pepper, mace, and cardamom pods
1 pound tart apples, peeled, cored, and chopped
½ pound pitted prunes, chopped
½ pound dried apricots, chopped
1 cup cider vinegar
1 cup brown sugar
1 teaspoon minced garlic
1½ teaspoons salt

1. Tie the spices together in a piece of washed cheesecloth.

2. Combine all the ingredients in a non-aluminum 4- to 6-quart saucepan. Simmer gently, stirring often, for about 1 hour. The chutney will become quite thick and toward the end of the cooking you may need to add a few tablespoons water to the pot to prevent scorching. As the fruits soften, mash them with the back of a wooden spoon. Discard the cheesecloth bag and cool the chutney. Transfer to glass jars and refrigerate. It will keep for weeks.

RHUBARB CHUTNEY

As with most chutneys and relishes, the proportions need not be absolute: a little more rhubarb or fewer onions will not alter its delicious and interesting taste.

Makes about 2 quarts

8 cups (about 3½ pounds) diced rhubarb
6 cups thinly sliced onions
6 cups brown sugar
4 cups cider vinegar
2 cups raisins
2 teaspoons ground cinnamon
1 teaspoon ground cloves
2 tablespoons grated fresh ginger or 2 teaspoons powdered ginger
Pinch of cayenne or crushed red pepper flakes

1. Combine all ingredients in a large heavy nonaluminum pan and, stirring often, simmer gently for about 1 hour, until mixture is thick.

2. When cool, transfer to glass jars and store, covered in the refrigerator. It will keep for months.

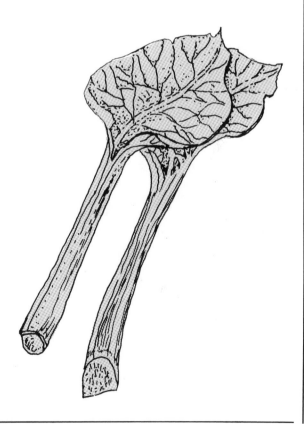

CRANBERRY CHUTNEY

This is not only delicious with ribs, but makes a real treat out of meatloaf, cold chicken, and even cottage cheese.

Makes about 2 quarts

1 pound cranberries
Thinly sliced peel of 1 lemon
1 cup brown sugar
½ cup raisins
½ cup white vinegar
1 large onion, sliced
1 teaspoon salt
1 teaspoon dry mustard
Cayenne
⅔ cup ginger preserves

1. In a large saucepan, combine with ¾ cup water everything but the ginger preserves. Over moderate heat, cook until the mixture thickens and the cranberries pop, 30 to 45 minutes.

2. Remove the saucepan from the heat and stir in the ginger preserves. When the mixture cools, transfer to covered jars and refrigerate. It will keep for months.

Desserts

APPLE BROWN BETTY

Choose apples that are firm and won't fall apart during cooking. Granny Smiths, Greenings, Northern Spys, Staymens, and Winesaps are good choices. Golden Delicious are okay: they hold their shape but don't have an interesting taste. Don't use McIntosh—they fall apart.

Serves 6

3–4 cups coarse fresh bread crumbs
8 tablespoons (1 stick) unsalted butter
3 pounds apples
1 lemon
¾ cup sugar
1 teaspoon cinnamon
½ teaspoon grated mace or nutmeg
Heavy cream or vanilla ice cream

1. Preheat the oven to 375° F.

2. Spread the bread crumbs on a jelly-roll pan or large cookie sheet and place in the oven. Stir them from time to time and remove when the crumbs are thoroughly dry and just start to take on color, about 15 minutes.

3. Melt the butter and combine with the lightly toasted bread crumbs.

4. Peel, core, and thinly slice the apples. You should have 6 to 7 cups of apples. Grate the peel of the lemon over the slices and then squeeze over the juice from half the lemon.

5. Combine the sugar, cinnamon, mace or nutmeg in a small bowl and stir into the apples.

6. To assemble the Brown Betty, butter a 2- to 2½-quart baking dish—a cylindrical charlotte mold is good. Place a shallow layer of the buttered crumbs on the bottom, then a layer of apples, continue alternating these layers, ending with a layer of crumbs.

7. Cover the dish with buttered aluminum foil (buttered-side down) and bake in the middle of the preheated oven for 30 minutes.

8. Remove the foil and return the Brown Betty to the oven for another 30 minutes. The apples should be tender, the juices syrupy, and the top brown.

9. Serve warm with heavy cream (whipped or not) or vanilla ice cream.

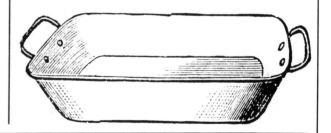

TYLER PIE

This dessert is said to have been the favorite of John Tyler, tenth president of the United States and a native of Orange County, Virginia. In some parts of the South it was called, simply, Sugar Pie. In the North, it was often made with maple syrup and that's my favorite and the one I give here. Tyler pie is a sweet, candylike dessert, and a little goes a long way.

Serves 6–8

Pastry
1½ cups unbleached, all-purpose flour
6 tablespoons chilled unsalted butter, cut into
      ¼-inch cubes
2 tablespoons (1 ounce) chilled lard or short-
      ening, cut into ¼-inch cubes
½ teaspoon salt
3–4 tablespoons ice water

Filling
1½ cups maple syrup
8 tablespoons (1 stick) unsalted butter
½ cup heavy cream
2 eggs plus 2 yolks
1 teaspoon vanilla extract
¼ teaspoon lemon extract
½ teaspoon cinnamon mixed with ½ tea-
      spoon grated nutmeg

1. In a large bowl or in the bowl of a standing electic mixer, combine the flour, butter, lard, and salt. With your fingertips or the paddle attachment of the mixer, work the flour and fats together until the mixture looks like coarse sand with particles the size of peas.

2. Add the ice water and mix with the fingertips of both hands. Even with an electric mixer you will have to get your hands into the dough at this point.

3. Shape the dough into a ball and place on a floured counter.

4. Taking lemon-size pieces of the dough (about 4 clumps in all), slide it with the heel of your hand, placed at an angle to the counter, 6 or so inches forward, flattening the pieces onto the counter.

5. When you've flattened all the dough, form it into a circle about an inch thick. Poke your finger into it: if the hole remains, you can use the dough immediately. If the hole closes, let the dough rest in the refrigerator for about an hour.

6. Preheat the oven to 400° F.

7. When the dough is ready, roll it out ⅛ inch thick and 13 or 14 inches in diameter.

8. Fit the dough into a well-buttered 9-inch pie plate; prick the bottom with the tines of a fork.

9. With kitchen shears, cut off the excess dough, leaving an overhang of about 1 inch. Roll this overhang forward—toward the center of the plate—forming a ropelike ring on the edge of the plate. Refrigerate for 1 hour.

10. Butter a sheet of aluminum foil large enough to cover the bottom and sides of the pastry and place it, buttered side against the pastry, in the shell. To be certain the pastry doesn't buckle, weight the shell with aluminum bits or beans or rice reserved for this purpose.

11. Bake the shell for 10 minutes, remove the foil, and bake for another 2 minutes. Remove from the oven and cool. Lower the oven temperature to 350° F.

12. Place the maple syrup, butter, and heavy cream in the top of a double boiler over simmering water. Heat, stirring, until the butter melts.

13. Beat the eggs until they thicken and look paler—about 5 minutes in the bowl of a standing electric mixer or with a portable hand mixer.

14. Pour the warm sugar mixture into the eggs, beating as your pour.

15. Add the extracts, mix, and pour into the partially baked shell.

16. Sprinkle with the cinnamon-nutmeg mixture and bake for 45 minutes, until a tester comes out dry and the top is puffy. The pie will sink as it cools.

MAPLE SYRUP

Sugar maple trees, the source of maple syrup and maple sugar, are grown in appreciable numbers only in the United States, Canada, Germany, and Japan. But only in the northeastern United States and adjacent areas of Canada is the weather just right to cause the sap to run in sufficient quantity to make tapping the trees worthwhile. It takes a minimum of 40 years before a sugar maple tree is large enough to be tapped. And it takes 35 to 40 gallons of sap to get one gallon of syrup.

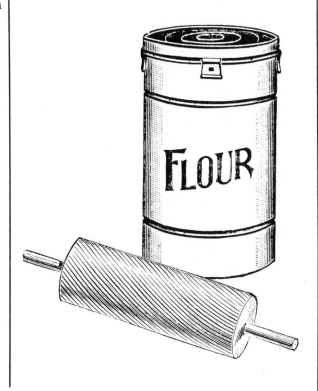

KEY LIME PIE

Very few Key lime pies are actually made with Key limes. The *Citrus aurantifolia* is small, almost perfectly round, and yellow inside. It is no longer commercially grown. So unless you have access to someone's private Key lime tree, make this pie with the Tahiti, Persian, or Bearss limes you find at your market.

Key lime pie was developed after the Civil War when supplies of fresh food were severely restricted in the devastated South. There was, however, plenty of sweetened condensed milk (first manufactured in 1858) and groves and groves of Key limes. The pie was originally made with a pastry crust because graham crackers were not created until many years after the pie was developed. If you prefer to make it as it was made 100 years ago, use the pastry recipe on page 104, baking for 15 to 20 minutes or until fully cooked and golden. Another modern change is the whipped cream topping; originally Key lime pie had a meringue topping because there was no available grazing land for cows and sweet cream was scarce.

Serves 6–8

Graham Cracker Crust
1 ¾–2 cups graham cracker crumbs
½ cup sugar (optional)
Nutmeg
5 ½ ounces (11 tablespoons) unsalted butter, melted and cooled to room temperature

Filling
6 egg yolks (either freeze the whites for later use or use 4 of them for meringue topping)
1 14-ounce can sweetened condensed milk
¾ cup freshly squeezed lime juice
Grated peel of 3 or 4 limes

Topping
1 cup heavy cream

or

Meringue
4 egg whites (left from filling ingredients)
Pinch of salt
4 tablespoons sugar

1. To make 2 cups of graham cracker crumbs, put 19 or 20 whole graham crackers (just short of two packets) in a blender or food processor and pulverize. Or put the graham crackers in a paper bag and pound with a rolling pin.

2. Combine all the crust ingredients in a bowl and mix with a wooden spoon. Place in a 9-inch pie plate. Using your thumbs, knuckles, and fingertips, gently press the crumbs to fill out the pie plate, going up the sides and around the rim. Refrigerate the crust while you prepare the filling.

3. Beat the egg yolks until they thicken and turn paler. This will take about 7 or 8 minutes with a standing electric mixer or a hand-held portable mixer.

4. Add the condensed milk and beat until smooth.

5. Stir in the lime juice and all but ½ teaspoon of peel. This mixture will be pale yellow. (Green filling, achieved only with the addition of food coloring, is definitely not authentic.)

6. Fill the prepared crust with the mixture and refrigerate or freeze for several hours.

7. Before serving, whip the cream and, with a spatula spread it over the filling. Or put the whipped cream in a pastry bag fitted with a plain or rosette tube and pipe it decoratively over the pie. Sprinkle the reserved lime peel over the topping.

8. If you want a meringue topping instead, beat the whites with a pinch of salt until they are frothy.

9. Add the sugar and continue beating until the whites are stiff but not dry.

10. Spread the meringue over the pie with a spatula, covering the surface completely. If you can handle a pastry bag (and the only way to learn is to keep doing it), fit it with a rosette tube and decoratively pipe the meringue over the pie, making sure the surface is completely covered.

11. Bake in a preheated 350° F. oven for 15 minutes, until the meringue is lightly brown.

12. Cool and refrigerate before serving.

VINEGAR PIE

This simple and unusual dessert comes, via Susan Bergholz and Bert Snyder, from Jim and Jean Hartbarger, owners of Jarrett House in Dillsboro, North Carolina.

Serves 6–8

1 partially baked pastry shell (see page 104)
8 tablespoons (1 stick) unsalted butter, melted and cooled
1–1½ cups sugar (depends on your sweet tooth)
2 tablespoons all-purpose flour
1 tablespoon vanilla extract
2–4 tablespoons white vinegar (depends on your sour tooth)
3 eggs
Fresh strawberries or raspberries for garnish

1. Preheat the oven to 300° F.

2. Combine all ingredients except the pastry shell and berries. Beat with a wire whisk.

3. Pour the filling into the partially baked shell and bake for 45 minutes.

4. Cool the pie on a rack and refrigerate for 2 to 3 hours before serving, garnished with strawberries or raspberries.

PAT BEAR'S PECAN PIE

This pecan pie is unusual because it uses no corn syrup and benefits from an unconventional crust. After baking, the pie can be frozen.

Chop the pecans in a wooden bowl with a crescent chopper; a food processor or blender releases too much oil from the nuts.

Serves 6

Pastry

6 ounces cream cheese
½ pound (2 sticks) unsalted buter
2 cups unbleached all-purpose flour

Filling

2 eggs
2 cups brown sugar
4 tablespoons (½ stick) unsalted butter, softened
2 cups (½ pound) chopped pecans
3 dozen (2½ ounces) pecan halves

Vanilla ice cream or whipped cream

1. In a large bowl or the bowl of a standing electric mixer, combine the pastry ingredients. If you use the electric mixer, the paddle attachment works best on this dough.

2. The dough will be very sticky but manageable. Place it on a heavily floured surface and roll out with a floured rolling pin to a thickness of ⅛ to ¼ inch.

3. Fold the dough over the rolling pin and place in a 9-inch fluted pie pan with a removable bottom.

4. Preheat the oven to 325° F.

5. Combine the eggs, brown sugar, butter, and chopped pecans and pour into the pastry. Decorate the circumference of the pie with the pecan halves.

6. Bake in the preheated oven for 40 minutes or until brown and firm. Cool on a rack.

7. Serve at room temperature with vanilla ice cream or whipped cream.

COOKIES. Any leftover cream-cheese dough can be frozen; or, you can sprinkle the rolled dough with sugar, cinnamon, ground cloves, and ground nuts. Cut into cookie shapes and bake at 325° F. for 12 to 15 minutes.

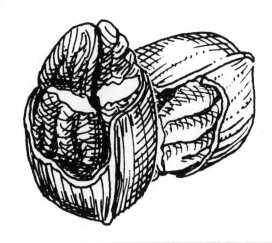

LEMON RING

When this lovely dessert emerges from the oven, there is sponge cake on top and custard on the bottom. It's magic!

Serves 6

3 tablespoons unsalted butter, softened
¾ cup sugar
½ cup all-purpose flour
Salt
⅓ cup lemon juice
Grated peel of 1 lemon
3 eggs, separated
1½ cups milk

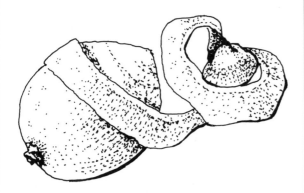

1. Preheat the oven to 350° F.

2. In the bowl of a standing mixer with the paddle attachment or in a large bowl with a wooden spoon, cream the butter with the sugar, flour, and salt. Mix in the lemon juice and grated peel. Set aside.

3. Heat (but don't boil) the milk in a small saucepan until small bubbles appear and a skin starts forming on the surface.

4. While milk is heating, beat the egg yolks until they thicken and turn paler in color. Slowly add the hot milk, beating constantly.

5. Add the egg-milk mixture to the sugar-flour mixture. Combine well.

6. Beat the egg whites until stiff but not dry and fold into the combined mixture.

7. Pour the batter into a buttered 6-cup ring mold. Place the ring mold in a larger pan with about ¾ inch of hot water on the bottom. Bake for 25 to 30 minutes, until the ring tests dry and there are golden spots on the top.

8. Let cool and then chill in the refrigerator. Unmold just before serving.

APPLE CRISP

Apple crisp is quickly prepared, delicious, and can be made all year round.

Serves 5–6

4–5 cups (about 2 pounds) sliced tart apples
Grated peel of 1 lemon
2 tablespoons lemon juice
½ cup flour
½ teaspoon ground cinnamon
¼ teaspoon ground cloves
¼ cup brown sugar
6 tablespoons unsalted butter, at room temperature
½ cup heavy cream
2 teaspoons sugar (optional)

1. Preheat the oven to 375° F.

2. Turn the apple slices into a buttered 9-inch pie plate. Grate the lemon peel directly over the apples, squeeze the juice, and toss 2 tablespoons with the apples.

3. Combine the flour, cinnamon, cloves, and brown sugar in a small bowl. Add the butter, cut into bits, and mix with your fingertips until the mixture is crumbly. Spread over the apples and bake for 45 minutes or until the top is brown and the juices are bubbling.

4. Serve warm, at room temperature, or chilled with heavy cream, in a pitcher or whipped and sweetened with 2 teaspoons sugar, if you like.

FRIED PIES

These pastries are usually made with dried fruit, though purées of fresh or canned fruits are also good.

Makes 16–20 pies

Fruit Filling

½ pound dried apples, prunes, peaches, pineapple, or apricots; or 2 cups thick, cooked, puréed fresh fruit
Sugar or honey
Spices: cinnamon, allspice, nutmeg, cloves, lemon peel

Pastry

2 cups flour
1 teaspoon salt
⅓ cup lard or shortening
5–6 tablespoons milk or water
1 beaten egg yolk (optional)
Confectioners' sugar

Vegetable oil for frying

1. Cover the dried fruit (any one or a combination) with boiling water and let stand for about 1 hour. Drain. Mash with a fork (do *not* use a food processor or blender) and add sugar or honey to taste—apricots will require more sweetener than prunes; pineapple may require none at all.

2. Simmer the sweetened fruit until it thickens. Add spice(s) to taste.

3. Put the flour and salt in a mixing bowl or the bowl of a standing electric mixer fitted with a pastry arm. Blend in the shortening or lard and mix with your fingertips or the pastry arm until the mixture forms particles the size of peas. Add only enough water or milk to form a stiff dough—it should be slightly moist. Refrigerate for at least 30 minutes.

4. Roll the dough to a thickness no greater than ⅛ inch. Using a floured cutter or the rim of a glass, cut rounds 3 to 4 inches in diameter.

5. Place 2 or 3 teaspoons of fruit on half the round, leaving the edge free.

6. Moisten the edges with water or beaten egg yolk diluted with 1 teaspoon water. Fold over and press the edges together with a fork or your fingertips, making sure the pies are completely sealed.

7. Fry the pies in 2 inches of oil heated to 375° F. (to test, a bread cube should fry golden in 40 seconds). Don't crowd the pan or the temperature of the fat will go down and produce greasy pies. When evenly brown, in a minute or two, remove the pies from the skillet and drain on paper towels. Continue frying, making sure the temperature of the oil remains at 375° F., until all the pies are fried.

8. Sprinkle with confectioners' sugar while still warm. The pies are best when just made, but they're good cold, too.

RICE PUDDING

Serves 6

4 cups milk
3 tablespoons unsalted butter
⅓ cup sugar
1 tablespoon grated orange peel
½ cup long-grain rice
3 egg yolks
4 tablespoons fresh orange juice
1 teaspoon vanilla extract
½ teaspoon ground cinnamon
Heavy cream

1. Combine 3 cups of the milk, the butter, sugar, and orange peel in a heavy saucepan. Bring to a boil and stir in the rice. Cook over very low heat, stirring from time to time, for about 45 to 50 minutes, or until most of the milk is absorbed, the mixture is creamy, and the rice is in danger of sticking to the bottom of the pan. Off the heat, gradually stir in the remaining cup of milk.

2. Preheat the oven to 300° F.

3. Stir the yolks with a fork just to mix. Add the orange juice and the vanilla extract. Slowly stir the yolks into the rice. Turn into a 6-cup buttered pan. Sprinkle with cinnamon. Place the rice in a larger pan with enough hot water to come halfway up the sides of the baking pan. Place in the middle of the oven and bake from 30 to 45 minutes or until a knife comes out clean. The pudding will cook faster in a shallow pan than in a deep one. Cool on a rack and serve warm, at room temperature, or chilled, with a pitcher of heavy cream.

PEACH COBBLER

Cobblers are related to pandowdies, grunts, slumps, and deep-dish pies. Cobblers traditionally have a cover of small, smooth rounds of biscuit dough, resembling cobblestones.

Serves 6

3 pounds peaches
3 tablespoons sugar
¼ teaspoon cinnamon
Nutmeg
½ teaspoon vanilla extract
Grated peel of 1 lemon

Biscuit Dough

¾ cup flour
1 teaspoon baking powder
Salt
3 tablespoons unsalted butter, at room temperature
1 egg, lightly beaten
2 tablespoons heavy cream

Whipped cream or vanilla ice cream

1. Drop the peaches into boiling water to cover for 1 minute to loosen their skins. Peel, pit, and slice, discarding any bruised or discolored areas. You should have 5 to 6 cups of sliced peaches.

2. Combine the peaches with the sugar, cinnamon, a few gratings of nutmeg, vanilla, and lemon peel grated over all. Mix well.

3. Place the peaches in a 6-cup baking dish. I use a round gratin pan, 8 inches in diameter and 2 inches high.

4. Preheat the oven to 400° F.

5. To make the biscuit dough, in a bowl combine the flour, baking powder, salt, and butter. Work with your fingertips or the paddle attachment of a standing mixer, until the mixture resembles coarse grain.

6. Add the egg and cream. Mix until smooth. You should have thick, sticky batter rather than dough. Drop this batter by teaspoonful over the peaches, leaving spaces between the dollops of batter, which should be about the size of silver dollars.

7. Bake in the preheated oven for 20 to 25 minutes, until the top is brown.

8. Serve warm or at room temperature with whipped cream or vanilla ice cream.

BLUEBERRY COBBLER. Combine 1½ quarts washed and picked-over blueberries with 4 tablespoons flour and 1 tablespoon lemon juice. Continue as for the peach cobbler. Serve with sour cream.

PLUM COBBLER. Combine 3 pounds pitted and halved fresh plums with 4 tablespoons sugar, 4 teaspoons grated orange peel, and ½ teaspoon ground allspice. Continue as for peach cobbler. Serve with whipped cream.

THE BEAR BROWNIE

These brownies are fudgelike rather than cakelike. They are *very* rich.

Makes 16 2" x 2" brownies

3 ounces unsweetened chocolate
2 ounces sweet chocolate
                    or
    5 ounces unsweetened chocolate
6 ounces (1½ sticks) unsalted butter, at room
    temperature
1 cup white sugar
1 cup brown sugar
4 eggs
1 teaspoon vanilla extract
¾ cup quick-mixing, enriched bleached flour
    (Wondra)

1. Preheat the oven to 350° F. Butter and flour a metal (brownies will burn in glass) 8-inch-square pan and set aside.

2. Melt the chocolate in the top of a double boiler over simmering water. Cool.

3. With a wooden spoon, or in the bowl of a standing electric mixer with the paddle attachment, cream the butter and sugars. Add the eggs and beat until they are fully incorporated. The mixture will be quite moist.

4. Add the vanilla and the flour. Mix well and make sure there are no lumps. Add the cooled chocolate. Combine until the mixture is all one color, without streaks.

5. Pour the batter into the prepared cake pan and bake in the preheated oven for 40 minutes. When done, the top will be cracked and dry but the batter will still shake a bit. Cool and refrigerate before cutting and serving.

Clean-up

It's disagreeable and most everyone hates it, but those pots and the oven must ultimately be confronted.

To clean your pots, put a few tablespoons of baking soda in the pot and pour in boiling water. Let the pot soak and then clean it out with a sponge or soft cloth. An abrasive pad will ruin the finish of some interiors. The baking-soda technique will restore the white color to enameled cast-iron interiors and will not harm tin-lined copper or aluminum. For cast iron, soak the pot in warm, soapy water. If you need some abrasion, pour in a few tablespoons of kosher salt and rub with paper towels. To prevent rusting, make sure you dry cast iron immediately after washing, either with a towel or over a low flame.

To clean the oven, put on rubber gloves; add a few tablespoons ammonia to a quart of warm water; put some liquid detergent on a sponge; dip the sponge into the water and clean the oven. You may need the help of steel wool. Avoid aerosol commercial oven cleaners; they will eventually rust away the thermostat. Any removable parts (the broiler pan, the racks, the pot holders) can be cleaned in the sink with boiling water, baking soda, and elbow grease. The clean-up chore becomes less punishing if you do it regularly.

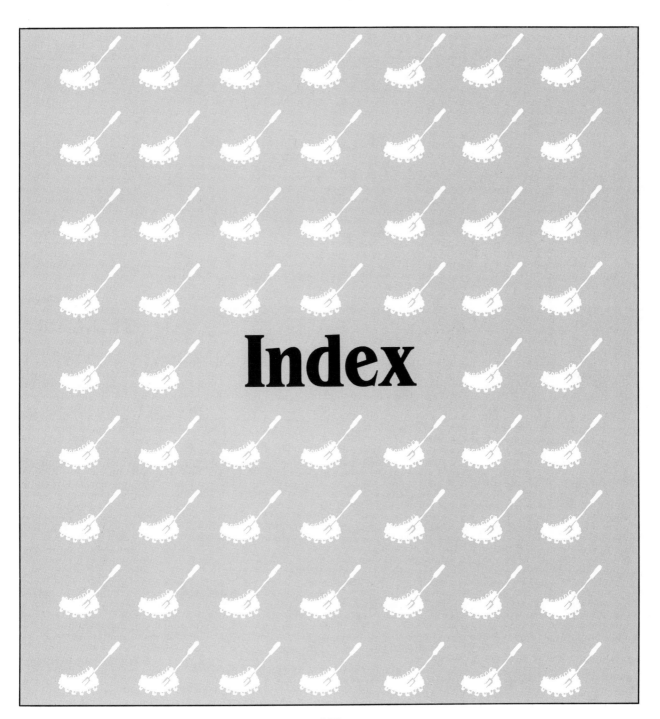

Index

A

Acorn Squash, ember cooking, 66
Alabama barbecues, 41
Appetizer Spareribs, Oriental Sweet-and-
    Sour, 40–41
Apple
  Brown Betty, 103
  Crisp, 111
  and Red Cabbage Slaw, 77
Aristotle, 75
Arizona Barbecued Ribs, 34

B

Baby backs, 13
Bacon
  -Potato Salad, 78
  and Turnips, 65
Barbara's Sautéed Peppers and Onions, 64
Barbecue
  origin of the word, 21
  Sauce, James C. Wright's, 27
Barbecued Ribs
  Arizona, 34
  Chinese, 25
  Citrus, 31
  Hot, 22
  Maple, 39
  Missouri, 28
  Molasses, 26
Beans
  Red, and Rice, 57
  see also Black-Eyed Peas
Bear Brownie, The, 115
Bear's, Pat, Pecan Pie, 109
Beet(s)
  about, 63
  Herbed, 63
  Salad, Creamy, 79

  Tangy Hot, 63
  Vinaigrette, 79
Biscuits
  Beaten, 87
  Buttermilk, 88
Black-Eyed Peas, Hoppin' John, 56
Black pepper, 37
Blueberry Cobbler, 114
Bourbon Ribs, 41
Braised Short Ribs, 44
Braziers, 14–15
Bread
  Corn, 89
  Sally Lunn, 91
  Spoon, 90
Bread and Butter Pickles, 95
Brownies, Bear, 115
Bulkogi (Korean Short Ribs), 42
Butel, Jane, 98
Buttermilk Biscuits, 88
Butternut Squash, ember cooking, 66

C

Cabbage
  about, 75
  see also Cole Slaw
Caper and Vinegar Sauce, Short Ribs with,
    46
Carrot
  Salad, 80
  and Turnip Salad, 80
Casserole
  Cornmeal and Cheese, 58
  Spareribs and Sauerkraut, 36–37
Charcoal briquettes, 15
Cheddar Spoon Bread, 90
Cheese and Cornmeal Casserole, 58
Chick Pea and Green Bean Salad, 82

Chili(es), 31
  Jam, 98
Chinese Barbecued Ribs, 25
Chutney
  Cranberry, 100
  Fruit, 98
  Rhubarb, 99
Citrus Barbecued Ribs, 31
Citrus-Chili Ribs, 30
Cleaning up, 117
Cobbler
  Blueberry, 114
  Peach, 114
  Plum, 114
Cole Slaw
  about, 76
  Creamy, 76
  Gale's, 77
  Miriam Weber's, 75
  Red Cabbage and Apple, 77
Columbus, Christopher, 37
Cookies, Cream-Cheese, 109
Corn
  about, 61
  ember cooking, 66
  Fritters, 70
  and Okra Creole, 69
  Relish, 97
  Salad, 83
  and Tomatoes, Stewed, 61
Corn Bread, 89
  Crackling, 89
  Jalapeño, 89
  Sticks, 89
Cornmeal
  about, 55, 90
  and Cheese Casserole, 58
  Mush, 55

  Mush, Fried, 55
Country Ribs, 13
Crackling Bread, 89
Cranberry Chutney, 100
Cream-Cheese Cookies, 109
Crown Roast of Spareribs, 35
Cumin seeds, toasted, 22

D
Desserts, 101–15
  Apple Brown Betty, 103
  Apple Crisp, 111
  Key Lime Pie, 106–7
  Lemon Ring, 110
  Pat Bear's Pecan Pie, 109
  Tyler Pie, 104–5
Devilled Short Ribs, 47

E
Easy Ribs, 29

F
Franklin, Benjamin, 90
Fried Pies, 112
Fruit
  Chutney, 98
  Pies, Fried, 112
  see also specific fruits

G
Gale's Cole Slaw, 77
Ginger-Soy Ribs, 29
Green Bean(s)
  and Chick Pea Salad, 82
  trimming and cooking, 82
Grilling ribs, 14–17

H

Hardwoods, 15
Hartbarger, Jim and Jean, 108
Hasty Pudding, 55
Herbed Beets, 63
Hippocrates, 37
Hoisin Sauce, 25
Hoppin' John, 56
Hot Barbecued Ribs, 22

J

Jalapeño chilies, 31
Jalapeño Corn Bread, 89
Jam, Chili, 98
James C. Wright's Barbecue Sauce, 27
Johnson, Lyndon, 27

K

Key Lime Pie, 106–7
Kidney Beans, Red, and Rice, 57
Korean Short Ribs (Bulkogi), 42

L

Lemon Potatoes, 52
Lemon Ring, 110

M

Maple Barbecued Ribs, 39
Maple Syrup, 105
Marinades, 13–14
Mesquite, 15
Miriam Weber's Cole Slaw, 75
Missouri Barbecued Ribs, 28
Molasses Barbecued Ribs, 26
Mop (sop), 13
Mustard Greens, 62
Mustard Ribs, 33

N

North Carolina Ribs, 21

O

Okra
    about, 68
    and Corn Creole, 69
    Fried, 68
Onion(s)
    Baked, 66
    Barbara's Sautéed Peppers and, 64
    Rings, Fried, 67
Orange Peel, Dried, 30
Oriental Sweet-and-Sour Appetizer
        Spareribs, 40–41
Oven, cooking ribs in the, 14

P

Pat Bear's Pecan Pie, 109
Patriae, Vindex, 90
Paula's Russian Ribs and Potatoes, 32–33
Peach Cobbler, 114
Peanut Sauce, Ribs with, 24
Pecan Pie, Pat Bear's, 109
Pepper, black, 37
Peppers, Bell, Barbara's Sautéed Onions and,
        64
Pickles
    Bread and Butter, 95
    Watermelon-Rind, 96
Pies
    Fried, 112
    Key Lime, 106–7
    Pat Bear's Pecan, 109
    Tyler, 104–5
    Vinegar, 108
Pigs, 22, 34

Plum Cobbler, 114
Poblano chilies, 31
Potato(es)
    -Bacon Salad, 78
    Cakes, 54
    ember cooking, 66
    Fried in Their Skins, 51
    Lemon, 52
    Mashed, 54
    Paula's Russian Ribs and, 32–33
    Stuffed, 53
Pudding, Rice, 113

R
Red Beans and Rice, 57
Red Cabbage and Apple Slaw, 77
Relish
    Corn, 97
    Tomato, 97
Rhubarb, Chutney, 99
Ribs
    Arizona Barbecued, 34
    Bourbon, 41
    buying, 13
    Chinese Barbecued, 25
    Citrus Barbecued, 31
    Citrus-Chili, 30
    Easy, 29
    Ginger-Soy, 29
    grilling, 14–17
    Hot Barbecued, 22
    Maple Barbecued, 39
    Missouri Barbecued, 29
    Molasses Barbecued, 26
    Mustard, 33
    North Carolina, 21
    oven cooking, 14
    with Peanut Sauce, 24

and Potatoes, Paula's Russian, 32–33
    short. *See* Short Ribs
    smoking, 15
    Southwestern-Style, 23
    Virginia, 28
    see also Spareribs
Rice
    about, 81
    Pudding, 113
    and Red Beans, 57
    Salad, 81
Roast of Spareribs, Crown, 35
Russian Ribs and Potatoes, Paula's, 32–33

S
Salads, 73–83
    Bacon-Potato, 78
    Beet, Creamy, 79
    Beets Vinaigrette, 79
    Carrot, 80
    Carrot and Turnip, 80
    Chick Pea and Green Bean, 82
    Cole Slaw, Creamy, 76
    Cole Slaw, Gale's, 77
    Corn, 83
    Red Cabbage and Apple Slaw, 77
    Rice, 81
Sally Lunn, 91
    Buns, 91
Sauce(s), 13–14
    Barbecue, James C. Wright's, 27
    Hoisin, 25
    Peanut, Ribs with, 24
    Vinegar and Caper, Short Ribs with, 46
Sauerkraut and Spareribs Casserole, 36–37
Serrano chilies, 31
Sesame seeds, toasted, 22

Short Ribs, 13
  Braised, 44
  Devilled, 47
  Korean (Bulkogi), 42
  Spicy, 45
  Tomato, 43
  Tzimmes, 48
  with Vinegar and Caper Sauce, 46
Smith, Landgrave T., 81
Smoking ribs, 15
Sop (mop), 13
Southwestern-Style Ribs, 23
Spareribs, 13
  Crown Roast of, 35
  Oriental Sweet-and-Sour Appetizer, 40–41
  and Sauerkraut Casserole, 36–37
  Stuffed, 38–39
  see also Ribs
Spicy Short Ribs, 45
Spinach, Creamed, 71
Spoon Bread, 90
  Cheddar, 90
Squash, ember cooking, 66
Stuffed Potatoes, 53
Stuffed Spareribs, 38–39
Sweet-and-Sour Appetizer Spareribs,
      Oriental, 40–41

T
Thackeray, William Makepeace, 91
Tomato(es)
  Relish, 97
  Stewed Corn and, 61
Turnips
  about, 65
  and Bacon, 65
  Buttered, 65
  and Carrot Salad, 80

  Mashed, 65
Tyler Pie, 104–5
Tyree, Mrs. Samuel, 28
Tzimmes, 48

V
Vegetables, 59–71
  Beets, Herbed, 63
  Beets, Tangy Hot, 63
  Corn and Okra Creole, 69
  Corn and Tomatoes, Stewed, 61
  Corn Fritters, 70
  ember cooking, 66
  Mustard Greens, 62
  Okra, Fried, 68
  Onion Rings, Fried, 67
  Onions, Baked, 66
  Peppers and Onions, Barbara's Sautéed, 64
  Spinach, Creamed, 71
  Turnips, Buttered, 65
  Turnips and Bacon, 65
Vinegar
  and Caper Sauce, Short Ribs with, 46
  Pie, 108
Virginia Ribs, 28

W
Watermelon-Rind Pickles, 96
Weber's, Miriam, Cole Slaw, 75
Wicker, Tom, 21
Wright, James C., 27
Wright's, James C., Barbecue Sauce, 27

About the Author

Susan R. Friedland, a writer and editor, lives and cooks in New York City where she was born. She has traveled near and far and eats well wherever she goes.